DAILY GRAMS: Guided Review Aiding Mastery Skills

GRADE 4

Author: Wanda C. Phillips

Published by ISHA Enterprises, Inc.
Easy Grammar Systems™
Post Office Box 25970
Scottsdale, Arizona 85255
www.easygrammar.com
© 2002

DAILY GRAMS: GUIDED REVIEW AIDING MASTERY SKILLS - GRADE 4
may be reproduced by the purchaser for student use only. Permission is not granted for district-wide, school-wide, or system-wide use. Reproduction for any commercial use is forbidden. Copyrighted materials. All rights reserved. No part of this book may be reproduced, stored in a retrieval system, or transmitted in any form or by any means, electronic, mechanical, recording, or otherwise.

CAPITALIZATION
Content and Sequence
Grade 4

Numbers indicate DAYS (page numbers) on which that concept is reviewed.

ABBREVIATIONS (Includes Initials and Postal Codes): 1, 12, 20, 27, 41, 42, 45, 53, 54, 60, 64, 71, 83, 97, 120, 122, 123, 137, 143, 153, 156, 158, 161, 164, 167, 172, 180

BRAND NAME: 58, 81, 126, 166

BUSINESS: 18, 24, 25, 27, 37, 44, 46, 60, 62, 63, 66, 68, 73, 100, 101, 115, 120, 133, 134, 141, 149, 161, 172, 175

CLOSING of a LETTER: 11, 27, 45, 71, 97, 137, 158, 180

CLUB/ORGANIZATION: 21, 44, 60, 69, 90, 96, 104, 108, 112, 130, 150

DAY of the WEEK: 3, 6, 9, 27, 43, 49, 55, 73, 146, 161

ETHNIC GROUP: 91, 170

FREEWAY/PARKWAY/Etc.: 17, 83, 120, 143

FRIENDLY LETTER: 9, 11, 27, 45, 54, 71, 97, 122, 137, 158, 180

GEOGRAPHIC PLACES:
    Bay: 64
    Beach: 38, 177
    Canyon: 71
    Cave: 168
    Continent: 5, 31, 85, 92, 98, 164
    Country: 5, 16, 19, 31, 74, 88, 97, 98, 100, 110, 131, 139, (141*), 142, 152, (166*), 168, 170, (1 (180*)
    County: 64
    Creek: 14
    Desert: 19, 71
    District: 114
    Forest (National): 103
    Island(s): 11, 50, 65, 168, 180
    Lake: 9, 163
    Mountain(s): 8, 10, 23, 117, 154
    Ocean: 39, 61, 95
    Park: 29, 32
    Park (National): 47, 118, 125
    Recreational Area: 94, 128
    River: 35, 154
    Sea: 142
    Spring(s): 75, 79, (97*), (117*)
    State: 4, 6-8, 12, 15, 16, 30, (54*), 57, (62*), (71*), (93*), (97*), 99, 116, (122*), 124, 125, (137*), 145, 158, 163, (177*), 179, (180*)
    Territory: 179
    Town/City: 4, 6, 12, 15, 42, 50, 54, 57, 71, 76, 97, 101, 114, 117, 124, 131, (133*), 137, (146*), 147, (148*), 151, 158, 163, 173, 179, 180
    Valley: 100
    Waterfall: 10, 30

GREETING of a LETTER: 9, 11, 27, 45, 54, 71, 97, 122, 137, 158, 180

HISTORICAL EVENT: 82, 89, 106, (119)*, 140, 174

HOLIDAY/SPECIAL DAY: 7, 13, 25, 48, 67, 75, 79, 93, 94, (108*), (115*), (123*), 130, (150*), 155, 171

LANGUAGE: 33, 90, 107, 155, 160, 170

MONTH: 3, 8, 11, 13, 19, 20, 42, 43, 54, 56, 71, 85, 92, 97, 104, 115, 122, 133, 137, 158, 163, 176, 180

NAMES OF PEOPLE: 1, 2, 6, 7, 9, 11, 12, 15, 17, 18, 20-22, 25, 27, 29, 33, 38-42, 45, 46, 52-56, 58, 60, 63-65, 67, 70-72, 79, 80, 83, 85, 88-92, 94-99, 101, 103, 106, 109, 112-114, 119, 120, 123, 126, 127, 137-139, 147-149, 152, 153, 155-158, 161, 163, 167, 169, 172-176, 179, 180

OUTLINE: 26, 51, 77, 102, 132, 159

POETRY (First Word of a Line): 34, 59, 84, 105, 135, 162

PRONOUN, I: 9, 46, 55, 68, 81, 88, 92, 113, 123, 126, 137, 158

PROPER ADJECTIVE: 35, 38, 62, 76, 82, 93, 95, 108, 115, 119, 123, 131, 133, 141, 142, 146, 148, 150-152, 166, 177, 180

QUOTATION (First Word): 55, 56, 58, 65, 70, 81, 85, 88, 89, 92, 99, 103, 113, 126, 127, 136, 145, 161, 163, 169, 172, 176

RELIGION: (76)*, 110, (131)*, (142)*, (152)*

SCHOOL/COLLEGE: 20, 23, 39, 104, 127, 155, 167

SENTENCE, FIRST WORD: 1-25, 27, 29-33, 35-50, 52, 53, 55-58, 60-64, 66-69, 71-76, 78-83, 86, 89-101, 104, 106-120, 123-128, 130, 131, 133, 134, 136-158, 160, 161, 163, 164, 166-177, 179, 180

SPECIAL EVENT: 32, 43, 56, 69, 78, 134, 151, 176

STREET/LANE/AVENUE/Etc.: 14, 15, 18, 37, 46, 53, 54, 57, 66, 67, 71, 97, 122, 137, 158, 167, 172, 180

STRUCTURES:
- Airport: 74
- Bridge: 113
- Building/Center: 153, 147
- Camp/Campground: 36, 157, 171
- Capitol: 156
- Castle: 107
- Church/Synagogue/
- Temple, Etc: 41, 72, 116
- Fort: 82, 174
- Hall: 86, 124, (173*)
- Historical Landmark: 50, 70, 86
- Hospital: 36, 123, 146
- House: 145
- Jail: 138
- Lighthouse: 61
- Mansion: 99
- Memorial: 114, 160
- Museum: 49, 144, 158, 173
- Palace: 169
- Ranch: 137

TITLE in PLACE of a NAME: 57, 109, 111, 163

TITLE of BOOKS and OTHER WORKS: 22, 28, 45, 52, 68, 80, 87, 111, 121, 129, 144, 149, 165, 178

TITLE with a NAME (*Captain, Mr., etc.*): 1, 2, 12, 17, 20, 25, 27, 33, 40, 41, 45, 53, 56, 60, 64, 67, 72, 79, 80, 83, 88, 89, 95, 97, 98, 106, 112, 119, 120, 123, 137, 138, 147, 148, 153, 156, 157, 161, 167, 172, 179

DO NOT CAPITALIZE:
- Animals: 29, 37, 47, 66, 92, 128, 179
- Career Choices: 24, 73, 101, 127, 160
- Directions: 17, 83, 100, 120, 154
- Diseases: 136, 153, 161
- Foods: 63, 66, 78, 93, 126, 141, 166, 171
- Games: 60, 78, 126
- Musical Instruments: 175
- Plants: 66, 67
- School Subjects: 53, 109, 167
- Seasons: 31, 47, 53, 76, 98, 137, 147, 152, 169, 175

*Parentheses ( ) designate a relationship to another category, also.

PUNCTUATION
Content and Sequence
Grade 4

Numbers indicate DAYS (page numbers) on which that concept is reviewed.

APOSTROPHE:
Contraction: 2, 4, 14, 16, 20, 22, 24, 28, 36, 42, 43, 45, 49, 54, 60, 65-67, 70, 74, 76, 77, 86, 92, 96, 99, 100, 102, 104, 118, 121, 127, 137, 138, 144, 158, 163, 165, 166, 169, 172-174

Plural Possessive: 63, 71, 85, 93, 113, 126, 130, 138, 140, 142, 145, 148, 154, 155, 158, 165, 167, 177, 179

Singular Possessive: 13, 15, 17, 19, 21, 27, 42, 54, 66, 70, 80, 88, 102, 105, 110, 117, 124, 127-129, 136, 143, 149, 173, 180

COLON:
List – Vertical and Within Sentence: 30, 51, 79, 101, 122, 151, 164, 176

Time: 11, 14, 28, 43, 57, 71, 93, 152, 179

COMMA:
Address Within Sentence *(I live at 1 Lu Lane, Reno, Nevada.)*: 17, 26, 37, 56, 80, 110, 123, 143, 170

Adjectives – Two Descriptive *(long, cold winter)*: 115, 117, 132, 145, 157, 179

Clarity: 31, 33, 61, 84, 97, 108, 136, 161

Closing of a Letter: 16, 24, 35, 65, 92, 95, 120, 134, 152, 167

Date *(January 1, 2000)*: 8, 13, 39, 52, 92, 120, 125, 134, 169

Date *(Monday, January 1)*: 8, 11, 13, 28, 43, 47, 88, 102, 113, 120, 124, 152, 165

Greeting of a Friendly letter: 12, 16, 24, 35, 52, 65, 84, 92, 105, 120, 134, 138, 152, 165, 169

Interrupter: 85, 93, 121, 128, 154, 156, 166

Introductory Word(s): 21, 22, 27, 36, 42, 54, 88, 99, 115, 127, 130, 155

Inverted Name: 27, 44, 64, 90, 119, 150

Items in a Series: 5, 10, 25, 35, 46, 51, 76, 89, 98, 101, 122, 126, 149, 151, 164, 176, 180

Noun of Direct Address: 6, 7, 14, 18, 34, 48, 49, 76, 98, 100, 118, 131, 137, 142, 146, 157, 166, 174, 176

Quotation Marks:
    After Name of Person Speaking *(Tate said,)*: 40, 41, 45, 57, 58, 62, 70, 73, 75, 104, 144, 148, 153, 158, 163, 172, 173, 177

    Within a Quotation *("I like you," said Bob.)*: 77, 78, 86, 87, 96, 153, 163, 172

Town/City with Country *(Athens, Greece)*: 32, 42, 67, 84, 114, 129, 161

Town/City with State *(Ajo, AZ)*: 7, 9, 17, 19, 22, 26, 37, 39, 52, 56, 80, 92, 110, 120, 123, 134, 143, 149, 152, 160, 169, 170, 178

EXCLAMATION POINT:
Exclamatory Sentence: 3, 15, 58, 62, 69, 74, 86, 131, 144, 147, 167, 174

Interjection: 3, 15, 58, 74, 131, 167, 174

HYPHEN:
Closely Related Words: 36, 78, 96, 104, 134, 156

Divided Word at End of Sentence: 38, 63, 84, 105, 134, 138, 165

Fraction: 25, 34, 48, 74, 99, 129, 140

Number: 20, 32, 60, 75, 92, 114, 120, 121, 151, 166

PERIOD:
Abbreviation (Including Initials): 1, 8, 12, 19, 29, 39, 44, 47, 49, 52, 56, 59, 63, 64, 83, 92, 94, 95, 109, 116, 123, 125, 132, 134, 137, 139, 152, 164, 174, 178

Outline: 23, 53, 82, 111, 141, 168

Sentence Ending: 2, 5, 8-11, 13-16, 19, 21, 22, 25-28, 31, 33-37, 40, 42-47, 51, 54, 56, 60, 61, 63-65, 67, 75-78, 80, 84-86, 88, 92-94, 96-102, 104-106, 108, 110, 113-115, 117, 118, 120-130, 132, 134, 136-138, 143, 145, 148, 149, 151-156, 158, 160, 161, 163-166, 169, 172, 176, 179, 180

QUESTON MARK: 4, 6, 7, 18, 20, 24, 32, 41, 48, 49, 57, 66, 69-71, 73, 78, 87, 89, 92, 100, 105, 106, 129, 140, 142, 146, 157, 158, 169, 170, 173, 177

QUOTATION MARKS:
  Direct Quotation:
    Occurring at Beginning (*"Go!" exclaimed Toni.*): 77, 78, 86, 87, 96, 106, 147
    Occurring at End *(Toni yelled, "Go!")*: 40, 41, 45, 57, 58, 62, 70, 73, 75, 104, 144, 148, 158, 173, 177
   Split: 153, 163, 172
  Title:
    Article: 72
    Chapter: 162, 175
    Essay/Report: 55
    Poem: 50, 81, 91, 107, 112, 133, 135, 171, 175
    Song: 81, 133, 155
    Story: 50, 68, 91, 103, 112, 135, 159

UNDERLINING:
  Name of Ship/Plane/Train: 100, 124, 146, 160, 162
  Title:
    Book: 50, 60, 68, 73, 81, 103, 107, 112, 133, 159, 162, 175
    Magazine: 50, 68, 91, 112, 171
    Movie: 55, 89, 159, 171, 175
    Newspaper: 72, 91, 133

Note: Concepts may be included under other headings as well. For example, interjections will also be reviewed within the "Grammar and Other Concepts" division. However, those have not been listed within this content and sequence.

GRAMMAR AND OTHER CONCEPTS
Content and Sequence
Grade 4

Numbers indicate DAYS (page numbers) on which that concept is reviewed.

ADJECTIVES:
    Adjective or Adverb Usage: 133, 144, 150
    Degrees: 89, 105, 107, 127, 145, 159, 180
    Descriptive: 4, 8, 12, 14, 38, 47, 54, 63, 83
    Limiting: 18, 28, 33, 34, 43, 44, 46, 54, 58, 61, 65, 70, 79, 85, 97, 109, 111, 125, 140, 141
    Limiting and Descriptive: 116, 142, 148, 163, 168

ADVERBS:
    Adverb or Adjective Usage: 133, 144, 150
    Degrees: 96, 108, 130, 143, 164, 172, 176
    Double Negatives: 70, 94, 115, 139
    How: 5, 23, 41, 67, 80, 84, 110, 137, 144, 152, 163, 167, 179
    To What Extent: 90, 119, 120, 149, 170, 179
    Well: 136, 144, 150, 176
    When: 6, 24, 40, 48, 68, 88, 132, 158, 163, 179
    Where: 7, 27, 40, 51, 74, 101, 110, 132, 158, 178

CONJUNCTIONS (Coordinating): 8, 32, 53, 78, 106, 129, 166, 173

DICTIONARY SKILLS:
    Alphabetizing: 1, 22, 47, 73, 99, 125, 151

DIFFICULT WORDS:
    Can/May: 23, 53, 81, 111, 122, 170
    It's/Its: 25, 54, 76, 97, 122, 146, 170, 179
    They're/Their/There: 10, 30, 54, 66, 91, 122, 146, 170, 179
    To/Two/Too: 40, 56, 76, 97, 122, 146, 170, 179
    You're/Your: 17, 30, 56, 76, 97, 146, 170, 179

FRIENDLY LETTERS:
    Envelopes: 102, 132, 161, 173
    Letter Parts: 58, 69, 92, 120, 137, 152, 169, 180

INTERJECTIONS: 28, 53, 82, 112, 139, 153, 166

NOUNS:
    Abstract/Concrete: 41, 64, 87, 107, 135, 160
    Common/Proper: 25, 38, 45, 52, 71, 75, 104, 124, 146, 156, 177
    Direct Object: 100, 114, 138, 147, 174
    Identification: 2, 3, 11, 20, 78, 105, 121, 151, 178
    Plurals: 14, 29, 34, 42, 49, 56, 62, 72, 93, 106, 131, 148, 175
    Possessives: 50, 59, 77, 88, 89, 98, 102, 113, 117, 122, 126, 155, 168

PREFIXES/ROOTS/SUFFIXES: 21, 48, 57, 69, 86, 92, 104, 114, 128, 138, 162

PREPOSITIONS:
    Identification of Prepositional Phrases: 15, 18, 22, (26*), (29*), (32*), 36, (46*), 55, (62*), 80, (82*), (86*), (91*), 96, (101*), 103*), (126*), (128*), (131*), (149*), 154, (156*), (158*), (165*), (169*), (175*)

Object(s) of the Preposition: 22, 36, 80, 96, 154
Prepositional Phrase Completion: 10
Prepositional Recognition: 13

PRONOUNS:
Antecedent: 165, 167
Compound: 6, 16, 27, 35, 63, 73, 118, 148
Nominative/Objective: 6, 16, 19, 27, 35, 37, 63, 68, 73, 93, 100, 118, 123, 148, 160, 171
    Used as Object: 37, 93, 127, 148, 160
    Used as Subject: 6, 16, 19, 27, 35, 63, 68, 73, 100, 118, 123, 148, (171*)
Possessives: 81, 99, 109, 113, 165, 167, 171

SENTENCE COMBINING: 1-180

SENTENCE TYPES: 7, 9, 17, 24, 37, 57, 77, 87, 95, 112, 143, 159, 176

SUBJECT/VERB AGREEMENT: 16, 19, 35, 45, 49, 50, 52, 76, 98, 119, 130, 134, 162

SUBJECT and VERB/VERB PHRASE IDENTIFICATION: 1, 3, 4, 9, 15, 20, 21, 26, 29, 32, 46, 59, 60, 62, 65, 74, 75, 79, 82, 85, 86, 91, 95, (100*), 101, 103, 108, 110, (114*), 115, 117, 121, 124, 126, 128, 129, 131, 133, 135, 138, 140-142, (147*), 149, 156, 158, 165, 169, 172, 174, 175
  Compound Subject: 59, 60, 79, 98, 103, 128, 158, 162, 169
  Compound Verb: 65, 85, 126, 129, 140, 156, 174

SYNONYMS/ANTONYMS/HOMONYMS: 5, 12, 26, 31, 42, 64, 94, 118, 134, 155, 178

VERBS:
Action: 13, 51
Compound Verb: 65, 85, 126, 129, 140, 156, 174
Contractions: 11, 39, 61, 90, 116, 136, 161, 174
Helping Verb or Main Verb: 30, 67
Helping Verbs: 36, 43, 44, 60, 66, 129, 149, 166
Helping Verbs in Verb Phrases: 71, 74, 75, 84
May/Can: 23, 53, 81, 111, 122, 170
Past Participle Construction of Irregular Verbs: (74*), 75, (95*), (110*), (117*), (124*), (133*), (135*), (142*), 147, 153, 164, 172
Regular or Irregular: 150, 157
Sit/Set, Lie/Lay, Rise/Raise: 72, 121, 126, 171
Subject/Verb Agreement: 16, 19, 35, 45, 49, 50, 52, 76, 98, 119, 130, 134, 162
Subject/Verb Identification: 1, 3, 4, 9, 15, 20, 21, 26, 29, 32, 46, 59, 60, 62, 65, 74, 75, 79, 82, 85, 86, 91, 95, (100*), 101, 103, 108, 110, (114*), 115, 117, 121, 124, 126, 128, 129, 131, 133, 135, 138, 140-142, (147*), 149, 156, 158, 165, 169, 172, 174, 175
Tenses: 31, 33, 39, 55, 83, 103, 123, 145, 147, 153, 164

*Parentheses ( ) designate a relationship to another category, also.

The purpose of **DAILY GRAMS: GUIDED REVIEW AIDING MASTERY SKILLS - GRADE 4** is to provide students with **daily** review of their language. Review of concepts helps to promote **mastery learning.**

This particular text offers more "teaching" than some *Daily Grams* books. However, *this text is not a teaching text;* it has been specifically designed for review. As in other *Daily Grams* texts, concepts are usually repeated within twenty-five to thirty days.

FORMAT

Note that each page is set up in this manner:

1. Sentence #1 always contains **capitalization**.

2. In sentence #2, students insert needed **punctuation**. You may want students to write this sentence, adding proper punctuation.

3. Numbers 3 and 4 address **general concepts**. You may wish to replace one of these items with material you are currently studying, especially if the concept provided has not yet been introduced.

4. Number 5 is always a **sentence combining**. Using the sentences given, students write a more intricate sentence. This helps students develop higher levels of writing. If you feel that the sentences given are too difficult, simply delete parts or replace them.

Note: An excellent teaching text for this level is *Easy Grammar: Grades 4 and 5*. To teach higher level sentence structures, *Easy Writing* is suggested. See the back of this text.

DAILY GRAMS: GUIDED REVIEW AIDING MASTERY SKILLS - GRADE 4

is designed as a guided review. There are 180 "GRAMS" in this book, one review per teaching day. **DAILY GRAMS** will take approximately **10 minutes** total time; this includes both completing and grading. (Don't be concerned if it take slightly longer.)

PROCEDURE

1. Students should be **trained** to do "GRAMS" immediately upon entering the classroom. Therefore, "GRAMS" should be copied, written on the chalkboard, or placed on a transparency for use with an overhead projector. (The projector may need to be adjusted to enlarge the print.)

2. Students will finish at different rates. Two ideas are suggested:

    A. Students read when finished.

    B. Students write in daily journals.

3. Go over the answers orally as a class. Discuss answers. (Example: Why is *America* capitalized?

4. In making students accountable for this type of activity, you may wish to take a quiz grade occasionally.

SUGGESTIONS

1. Make transparencies and file them. These can be used each year. Simply draw that day's "GRAMS" from your file.

2. You may choose to purchase a workbook for each student or to make copies for each student. A transparency is still needed. Students usually learn more by seeing the answers.

3. Solicit as much **student response** as possible. Keep the lesson lively!

4. If possible, allow students to write the sentence combining on the board. Use this for class "editing" and **praise**!

5. As one progresses through this book, some of the sentence combinings become longer and more complex. This may necessitate an adaptation to your own teaching style and to your students' needs.

Note: Student **workbooks** are available and will save you valuable time. These contain the same daily reviews as the teacher text. The introductory pages and the answers are not included in the workbooks.

DAY 1

CAPITALIZATION:

Capitalize a name.
Example: Patty

Capitalize initials.
Example: P. T. Lutz

Capitalize a title with a name.
Examples: Mr. Scott   Mayor Hill   Uncle Peter

1. have dr. and mrs. c. winston visited lately?

   Have Dr. and Mrs. C. Winston visited lately?

PUNCTUATION:

Place a period after an abbreviation.

Write the abbreviation:

2. A. Avenue - *Ave.*   C. Mister - *Mr.*   E. inch - *in.*
   B. gallon - *gal.*   D. foot - *ft.*   F. Street - *St.*

ALPHABETIZING:

Write these words in alphabetical order:

3. dream   dart   cream   egg   breath

   (a) *breath*   (d) *dream*
   (b) *cream*   (e) *egg*
   (c) *dart*

SUBJECT/VERB:

The subject of a sentence tells <u>who</u> or <u>what</u> the sentence is about.
The verb tells what <u>is</u> (<u>was</u>) or what <u>happens</u> (<u>happened</u>).

Underline the subject once and the verb twice.

4. Suddenly Janet sneezed.

SENTENCE COMBINING:

5. Her brother is making cookies.
   They are for a bake sale.

   Her brother is making cookies for a bake sale.

DAY 2

CAPITALIZATION:

Capitalize a title if it appears with a name.
Example: Grandma Rich

Do not capitalize a title if it appears alone.
Example: I like my grandma.

1. has uncle mike met miss diaz?

   Has Uncle Mike met Miss Diaz?

PUNCTUATION:

Place a period at the end of a declarative sentence (statement).
Place a period at the end of an imperative sentence (command).

2. Don't go*!* or *Don't go.*

PARTS OF SPEECH: VERBS

A contraction combines two words and omits a letter or letters. An apostrophe (') is placed where the letter or letters have been left out.   Example: we are = we're

Write the contraction:

3. A. is not - *isn't*
   B. they are - *they're*
   C. cannot - *can't*

PARTS OF SPEECH: NOUNS

A noun names a person, place, or thing.

4. Write a noun that names a person: *boy, Nels, girl, Jos*

SENTENCE COMBINING:

5. A book is on the table.
   It is a library book.

   1.) *A library book is on the table*
   2.) *A book that is on the table is from the library*

DAY 3

CAPITALIZATION:

Capitalize the days of the week.
    Example: Sunday

Capitalize the months of the year.
    Example: January

1. their party is on the last saturday in july.

   Their party is on the last Saturday in July.

PUNCTUATION:

Place an exclamation point (!) after an interjection (word that shows emotion).
Place an exclamation point at the end of an exclamatory sentence (one that shows emotion).

2. Wow I won

   Wow! I won!

SUBJECT/VERB:

The subject of a sentence tells <u>who</u> or <u>what</u> the sentence is about.
The verb tells what <u>is</u> (<u>was</u>) or what <u>happens</u> (<u>happened</u>).

Underline the subject once and the verb twice:

3. A <u>band</u> <u>marches</u> every morning.

PARTS OF SPEECH: NOUNS

A noun names a person, place, or thing.

4. Write a noun that names a thing: *coat*

SENTENCE COMBINING:

5. Mark is sick today.
   Mark had to stay home.

   1) *Mark is sick today so he had to stay home.*
   2) *Mark stayed home today because he is sick.*

DAY 4

CAPITALIZATION:

Capitalize the name of a geographic place.
Examples:
town or city - Abileen
state - Utah

1. my aunt lives in san diego, california.

   My aunt lives in San Diego, California.

PUNCTUATION:

Place a question mark (?) at the end of an interrogative sentence.

2. Arent we leaving soon

   Aren't we leaving soon?

PARTS OF SPEECH: ADJECTIVES

Some adjectives describe; they are called descriptive adjectives.
Write a descriptive adjective in each blank:

3. Two ___*blue*___ cars were parked by the ___*old*___ house.

PARTS OF SPEECH: VERBS

Underline the subject once and the verb twice:

4. Our dog licks us.

SENTENCE COMBINING:

5. The basket is broken.
   The basket is green and pink.

   The green and pink basket is broken.

Week 2
DAY 5 (4 day week)

CAPITALIZATION:

Capitalize the name of a geographic place.

Examples:
- **country** - Canada
- **continent** - North America

1. the country of finland is in europe*.

   *name of a continent

   The country of Finland is in Europe.

PUNCTUATION:

**Place a comma after three or more items in a series.
Do not place a comma after the last item.**

Example: I saw goats, cows, and chicks at a farm.

2. Mira Frank and Chan were first

   Mira, Frank and Chan were first.

SYNONYMS:

Synonyms are words with similar meanings.
Circle a synonym for the boldfaced word:

3. **respect:**   a) dislike   **b) admire** ⃝   c) despise

PARTS OF SPEECH: ADVERBS

Adverbs often tell how.
Circle any adverbs that tell <u>how</u>:

4. She did her work (carefully).

SENTENCE COMBINING:

5. The telephone rang.
   Ted answered it.

   The telephone rang and Ted answered it.

DAY 6

CAPITALIZATION:

1. carissa drove to austin, texas, last tuesday.

PUNCTUATION:

Place a comma after a noun of direct address. This is a person to whom someone is speaking.

Example: Lori, sit here.

2. Tom can you play

PARTS OF SPEECH: ADVERBS

Adverbs often tell when.

Circle any adverbs that tell <u>when</u>:

3. Our picnic is today.

PARTS OF SPEECH: PRONOUNS

Pronouns take the place of nouns.
I, he, she, we, they, you, it, and *who* are pronouns that can serve as a subject.

Circle the correct pronoun:

4. Jasper and _____ (me, I) are right.

SENTENCE COMBINING:

5. Tama's bike had a flat tire.
   Tama fixed her flat tire.

_____

_____

DAY 7

CAPITALIZATION:

Capitalize the name of a holiday or special day.

Examples:
holiday - Labor Day
special day - St. Patrick's Day

1. susan's family went to hawaii last christmas.

PUNCTUATION:

Place a comma between a town or city and a state.

Example: Gunder, Iowa

2. Mary have you been to Denver Colorado

PARTS OF SPEECH: ADVERBS

Adverbs often tell where.

Circle any adverbs that tell <u>where</u>:

3. A child fell down.

SENTENCE TYPES:
A declarative sentence makes a statement.
An interrogative sentence asks a question.

Write the sentence type:

4. Are you leaving? _____

SENTENCE COMBINING:

5. The dish was dropped.
   The dish broke into many pieces.

_____

_____

DAY 8

CAPITALIZATION:

Capitalize the name of a geographic place:

Examples:

    ocean - Pacific Ocean   **island** - Egg Island
    river - Snake River   **mountain** - Brock Mountain
    lake - Soda Lake   **canyon** - Grand Canyon
    bay - Bua Bay   **beach** - Stone Beach

1. they visited the ozark mountains in missouri in august.

PUNCTUATION:

**Place a comma between the number for a day and the year in a date.
Place a comma between a day and a date.**

    Example: Tuesday, October 23, 2001

2. He was born on Oct 20 1980

PARTS OF SPEECH: CONJUNCTIONS

Write the coordinating conjunction that rhymes with each word:

3. A. sand - _____   B. more - _____   C. mutt - _____

PARTS OF SPEECH: ADJECTIVES

Some adjectives describe; they are called descriptive adjectives.

Circle any descriptive adjectives:

4. White fluffy clouds were painted above the iron bed.

SENTENCE COMBINING:

5. Joe's mom is a dentist.
    Joe's dad is a dentist.

_____

_____

DAY 9

CAPITALIZATION:

Capitalize the first word of a greeting (salutation) of a friendly letter.

Example: Dear Susie,

1. dear marco,

    terry and i will visit fish lake next thursday.

    brian

PUNCTUATION:

2. Tara and I visited Anaheim California

SENTENCE TYPES:

A declarative sentence makes a statement.
An interrogative sentence asks a question.

Write the type of sentence:

3. A. Will you go?   _____

    B. The sun is bright. _____

SUBJECT/VERB:

Underline the subject once and the verb twice:

4. That horse chews hay.

SENTENCE COMBINING:

5. The roses were blooming.
    The daisies were not blooming.

    _____

    _____

DAY 10

CAPITALIZATION:

Capitalize the name of a geographic place.

Examples: **valley** - Round Valley   **cape** - Cape Horn
springs - Holly Springs   **dam** - Beaver Dam
creek - Clear Creek   **point** - Fairbanks Point
gulf - Gulf of Biscayne   **waterfalls** - Miners Falls

1. is bighorn falls near marsh peak?

PUNCTUATION:

2. Maria Frank and Laylah left early

DIFFICULT WORDS:

<u>They're</u> is a contraction for they are.   Example: They're finished.
<u>There</u> is an adverb telling where.   Example: Stand there.
<u>Their</u> is a possessive pronoun.   Example: I'm their cousin.

Circle the correct word:

3. (They're, There, Their) dad is a carpenter.

PARTS OF SPEECH: PREPOSITIONS

Prepositions are words that appear with other words to form prepositional phrases. These phrases add details or more information. Common prepositions are *at, by, for, from, in, on, to,* and *with*.

Examples: The teenager stood <u>by his father</u>.
The message <u>on the card</u> was scribbled.

Finish this sentence:

4. We laughed **at** _____.

SENTENCE COMBINING:

5. Jason mailed a letter.
He did it for his dad.

_____

DAY 11

CAPITALIZATION:

Capitalize the first word of a closing of any letter.

Example: Truly yours,

1. dear janny,
   we are going to grand island in june.
       your friend,
       tony

PUNCTUATION:

Place a colon between the numbers for the hour and minutes.

Example: We are arriving at 4:15 tomorrow.

2. We took our pet to the clinic at 10 15 on Monday August 3

PARTS OF SPEECH: VERBS

Write the contraction:

3. A. should not - _____   D. I am - _____
   B. are not - _____   E. I have - _____
   C. he will - _____   F. will not - _____

PARTS OF SPEECH: NOUNS

A noun names a person, place, or thing.

Circle any nouns:

4. My aunt brought her puppy to our home.

SENTENCE COMBINING:

5. The chalkboard was dusty.
   Two students washed it.

_____

_____

DAY 12

CAPITALIZATION:

1. the family of dr. begay visited blackstone, virginia.

PUNCTUATION:

Place a comma after the greeting of a friendly letter.
Example: Dear Marco,

2. Dear Mrs Tate

PARTS OF SPEECH: ADJECTIVES

Circle any adjectives that tell <u>what kind</u>:

3. Cold sandwiches and chocolate cake were served.

SYNONYMS/ANTONYMS/HOMONYMS:

Antonyms are words with opposite meanings.
Example: fresh - wilted

Circle the antonym of the boldfaced word:

4. **fuzzy:**   a) clear   b) blurred   c) hazy

SENTENCE COMBINING:

5. Jane's brother is on the swim team.
   Jane's brother is ten years old.

   _____

   _____

DAY 13

CAPITALIZATION:

1. we celebrated memorial day at a park in may.

PUNCTUATION:
Place an apostrophe (') before the s if the word shows ownership and is singular (one).
Example: Joy's shoe

2. My aunts graduation party was Saturday June 17 2000

PARTS OF SPEECH: PREPOSITIONS
Unscramble these prepositions:

3. A. ot - _____   D. no - _____   G. yb - _____
   B. ta - _____   E. fro - _____   H. twih - _____
   C. ni - _____   F. mfor - _____   I. pu - _____

PARTS OF SPEECH: VERBS
Some verbs show action.
Example: Micah <u>threw</u> a horseshoe.
Some verbs make a statement.
Example: Janice <u>likes</u> board games.
Place a √ if the underlined verb shows action:

4. A. ____ Barb <u>hammered</u> a nail into the floor.
   B. ____ We <u>dragged</u> the large rug outside.
   C. ____ Their mom <u>is</u> very funny.

SENTENCE COMBINING:

5. A carriage was pulled by a horse.
   The carriage was decorated with flowers.

_____

_____

DAY 14

CAPITALIZATION:

    Capitalize the name of a street, avenue, lane, freeway, or other roadways.
        Example: Locust Road

1. we took old mill lane to attend a picnic on turkey creek.

PUNCTUATION:

2. Molly our bus wont leave until 7 00

PARTS OF SPEECH: ADJECTIVES

  Circle any adjectives that tell <u>what kind</u>:

3. Big blue balloons were hanging there.

PARTS OF SPEECH: NOUNS

    Plural means more than one.
    Most plurals are formed by adding <u>s</u>.

    Place a √ if the plural is formed by adding <u>s</u>:

4. A. _____ chair
   B. _____ man
   C. _____ raisin

SENTENCE COMBINING:

5. The Spanish brought figs to America.
   The Spanish brought dates to America.
   The Spanish brought citrus fruits to America.

_____

_____

DAY 15

CAPITALIZATION:

Do not capitalize a direction (north, south, east, west, northeast, northwest, southeast, southwest).

Example: They live west of Davis Pond.

However, capitalize a direction when it appears with the name of a geographic place.

Examples: North Central Avenue
West Virginia

1. the smith family lives at 22 east ball street, reno, nevada.

PUNCTUATION:

2. Yikes Timmys snake is lost

SUBJECT/VERB:

Underline the subject once and the verb twice:

3. My cat sneezes.

PARTS OF SPEECH: PREPOSITIONS

A prepositional phrase begins with a preposition and ends with a noun or pronoun.

Examples: **down** the road
to me

Circle the prepositional phrase:

4. We ate supper at a diner.

SENTENCE COMBINING:

5. Ken skied for two hours.
   Ken fell three times.

_____

_____

DAY 16

CAPITALIZATION:

1. was virginia the first state in the united states of america?

PUNCTUATION:

Place a comma after the closing of a letter.

> Example: Love,
> Trena

2. Dear Ben
   Ill meet you soon
      Your friend
      Mickey

SUBJECT-VERB AGREEMENT:

**The verb must agree with the subject.
In present time, if the subject is singular (one), add s to the verb (unless the subject is *you* or *I*).**

> Example: Her <u>brother</u> like**s** to drive.

Underline the subject once. Place two lines under the verb that agrees with the subject:

3. Their pig (oink, oinks) often.

PARTS OF SPEECH: PRONOUNS

Pronouns take the place of nouns.

4. A. Bo and _____ are coming with you.
             (your name)
   B. Bo and _____ (I, me) are coming with you.

SENTENCE COMBINING:

5. In colonial days, carrot juice was often added to butter.
   Salt was also often added to butter.

   _____

   _____

DAY 17

CAPITALIZATION:

1. senator tang drove north on the santa ana freeway.

PUNCTUATION:

Place a comma after the street address and after the town or city if an address is written within a sentence.

       Example: He lives at 12 Skylar Street, Boonville, New York.

2. Does Sallys uncle lives at 4 Cedar Road Cleveland Ohio

DIFFICULT WORDS:

   <u>You're</u> **is a contraction for you are.**   Example: You're next!
   <u>Your</u> **is a possessive pronoun.**   Example: What's your name?

Circle the correct word:

3. (Your, You're) note pad is on the floor.

SENTENCE TYPES:

Is the following sentence declarative or interrogative?

4. Will you help me? _____

SENTENCE COMBINING:

5. The television is broken.
   David will repair it after school.

_____

_____

DAY 18

CAPITALIZATION:
   Capitalize the name of a business.
      Example: Mott Motor Company

1. matt's savings account is at prime bank on colt street.

PUNCTUATION:

2. Miss Stoner may I carry your box

PARTS OF SPEECH: PREPOSITIONS
   Circle any prepositional phrases:

3. Is that letter from your friend?

PARTS OF SPEECH: ADJECTIVES
   There are three limiting adjectives called articles.
   Circle the three articles:

4. my   a   but   the   dirty   an   do

SENTENCE COMBINING:

5. The children wore bathing suits.
   The children wore sandals.
   The children also wore hats.

_____

_____

DAY 19

CAPITALIZATION:

Capitalize the name of a particular place.

Examples:

gap	- Cumberland Gap	**park**	- Gateway Park
point	- Sunset Point	**forest**	- Sherwood Forest
desert	- Mojave Desert	**harbor**	- Stone Harbor
county	- Pima County	**trail**	- Santa Fe Trail

1. they went through the yuma desert in mexico in april.

PUNCTUATION:

2. Bobs mother flew to St Augustine Florida

PARTS OF SPEECH: PRONOUNS

Circle the correct usage:

3. (Me and Josh, Josh and I, Josh and me) will do it.

SUBJECT-VERB AGREEMENT:

**The verb must agree with the subject.
In present time, if the subject is singular (one), add s (or *es*) to the verb (unless the subject is *you* or *I*).**

Example: My sister helps me.

Underline the subject once. Place two lines under the verb that agrees with the subject:

4. His tie (match, matches) his socks.

SENTENCE COMBINING:

5. A deer ate grass in the meadow.
   The meadow was wide and green.

_____

_____

DAY 20

CAPITALIZATION:

Capitalize the name of a school, college, library, or hospital.

Examples: **school** - Keys Elementary School
college - Oxford University
library - Washington Library
hospital - St. Mary's Hospital

1. mr. jay began attending wells college in september.

PUNCTUATION:

Use a hyphen between two-word numbers between 21 and 99.
Example: thirty-four

2. Cant we spend twenty five dollars on their gift

SUBJECT/VERB:

Underline the subject once and the verb twice:

3. We clapped our hands.

PARTS OF SPEECH: NOUNS

A noun names a person, place, or thing.

Circle any nouns:

4. Put your shirt in the closet.

SENTENCE COMBINING:

5. A teacher spoke about Indian life.
The teacher is from Utah.

_____

_____

DAY 21

CAPITALIZATION:

1. does steve sax still play for the los angeles dodgers*?

*name of a baseball team

PUNCTUATION:

Place a comma after <u>yes</u> or <u>no</u> at the beginning of a sentence. These are called introductory words.

Example: No, I won't!

2. Yes Tammys dog had puppies

PARTS OF SPEECH: VERBS

Verbs often show action.

Underline the subject once and the verb twice:

3. Her horse lifted its head.

PREFIXES/ROOTS/SUFFIXES:

A root is any "word" without a part added at the beginning or end.

Examples: trying = **try** + ing   subway = sub + **way**
                     (root) (suffix)   (prefix) (root)

4. The root of **boldness** is _____.

SENTENCE COMBINING:

5. The toddlers were playing with toy cars.
   The cars were yellow and red.

_____

_____

DAY 22

CAPITALIZATION:

Capitalize the first word, the last word, and all important words in a title. Do not capitalize *a*, *an*, *the*, *and*, *but*, *or*, or *nor* unless it is the first or last word.
Examples: "Tiny but Strong"
"The Big Hawk"

1. he checked out clifford takes a trip* at pinto library.

*name of a book

PUNCTUATION:

2. No my uncle doesnt live in Orlando Florida

ALPHABETIZING:

Write these words in alphabetical order:

3. strut   vent   sung   track   smoke

   (a) _____ (d) _____
   (b) _____ (e) _____
   (c) _____

PARTS OF SPEECH: PREPOSITIONS

A prepositional phrase begins with a preposition and ends with a noun or pronoun. That noun or pronoun is called the object of the preposition (O.P.).
                                           O.P.
Examples: Jason sat **with his family**.   O.P.
A postal worker handed a box **to me**.

Circle the prepositional phrase. Box the object of the preposition.

4. Dinner is in the oven.

SENTENCE COMBINING:

5. An eagle is perching on a limb.
   The limb is part of a dead tree.

   _____

   _____

DAY 23

CAPITALIZATION:

1. is penn state university located in the nittany mountains?

PUNCTUATION:

Place a period after numbers and letters of an outline.

    Example: I. Ropes
                        A. Hemp
                        B. Wire

2.   I Idaho
      A Land
      B People

PARTS OF SPEECH: VERBS

    Can means to be able to.   Example: He can make pottery.
    May asks or states permission.   Example: May I stay with you?

    Circle the correct verb:

3. You (can, may) change the channel.

PARTS OF SPEECH: ADVERBS

    Circle any adverbs telling how:

4. She did her work fast but carefully.

SENTENCE COMBINING:

5. A basket is hanging on her patio.
   The basket contains flowers.
   The flowers are bright yellow.

_____

_____

DAY 24

CAPITALIZATION:

Do not capitalize a career choice.

Example: He is a teacher.

1. a secretary at fann company ordered glass for the window.

PUNCTUATION:

2. Dear Vivian

    Hows the summer going for you

    A friend always
    Candy

PARTS OF SPEECH: ADVERBS

Circle any adverbs that tell <u>when</u>:

3. We planned to arrive early but arrived late.

SENTENCE TYPES:

An imperative sentence states a command.
An exclamatory sentence shows excitement. It ends with an exclamation point (!).

Write the type of sentence:

4. A. You're the winner!   _____

   B. Pass the butter.   _____

SENTENCE COMBINING:

5. The trees were dropping their leaves.
   It was autumn.

   _____

   _____

DAY 25

CAPITALIZATION:

1. on valentine's day, aunt nina received a gift from savoy candy store.

PUNCTUATION:

Use a hyphen in fractions.
Example: two-thirds

2. We need two eggs butter and one half cup of milk for the cookies

DIFFICULT WORDS:

It's is a contraction for it is.   Example: It's cold in this room.
Its is a possessive pronoun.   Example: A finch is in its cage.

Circle the correct word:

3. The dog wagged _____ (it's , its) tail.

PARTS OF SPEECH: NOUNS

A common noun names any person, place, or thing. Example: animal

A *type* is still a common noun. Example: seal

A proper noun is specific. A proper noun is capitalized.
Example: common - mountain
proper - Mt. Humphreys

Capitalize any proper noun:

4. A. friend   C. iowa   E. valley

   B. elizabeth   D. november   F. monday

SENTENCE COMBINING:

5. Lily likes to ski.
   Lily likes to sled.
   Lily likes to ice skate.

_____

_____

DAY 26

CAPITALIZATION:
Capitalize the Roman numerals (I, II, III, IV, V, etc.) and letters for each major division in an outline. Capitalize the first word of each line.

Example: I. Pets
                    A. Barn pets
                    B. House pets

Capitalize the outline:

1. i. desert animals
      a. rattlesnakes
      b. turtles

PUNCTUATION:

2. Our new address is 12 Link Drive Biglerville Pennsylvania   17307

SYNONYMS:
Synonyms are words with similar meanings.

Circle a synonym for the boldfaced word:

3. **flawless:** a) blemished   b) stained   c) perfect

SUBJECT/VERB:
A prepositional phrase will usually not be the subject or verb. Therefore, crossing out any prepositional phrases helps to simplify the process of finding the subject and verb.

Example: The <u>lady</u> <u><u>waved</u></u> ~~to her friend~~.

Cross out the prepositional phrase. Underline the subject once and the verb twice:

4. Those trees sway in the wind.

SENTENCE COMBINING:

5. The Mayans had a system of writing.
    The Mayans also had a 365-day calendar.

_____

_____

DAY 27

CAPITALIZATION:

Remember:

**Capitalize the first word of a greeting (salutation) of a letter.
Capitalize the first word of a closing of a letter.**

1. dear molly,

    mrs. bole will take us to blackhawk mall on thursday.

                    your friend,

                    chan

PUNCTUATION:
Use a comma to invert a name.

   Example: Welk, Diana

2. Yes his name appears in the churchs directory as Lima Steve

PARTS OF SPEECH: PRONOUNS
Circle the correct pronoun:

3.   May Barb and _____ (me, I) go to the library?

PARTS OF SPEECH: ADVERBS
Circle any adverbs that tell <u>where</u>:

4.   A bird darted here and there.

SENTENCE COMBINING:

5.   The butterfly is black and white.
     The butterfly is sitting on a tiny daisy.

_____

_____

DAY 28

CAPITALIZATION:

Remember:

Capitalize the first word, the last word, and all important words in a title. Do not capitalize <u>a</u>, <u>an</u>, <u>the</u>, <u>and</u>, <u>but</u>, <u>or</u>, or <u>nor</u> unless it is the first or last word.

Capitalize these titles:

1. A. <u>monkey tales</u>

    B. "the brave knight"

PUNCTUATION:

2. Well arrive at 9 00 on Saturday July 14

PARTS OF SPEECH: ADJECTIVES

Circle any adjectives that tell <u>how many</u>:

3. In the two classes, there were thirty children.

PARTS OF SPEECH: INTERJECTIONS

An interjection is a word or phrase (group of words) that shows excitement or strong emotion.

       Example: **Whoa!** Slow down!

Circle the interjection:

4. Hurray! I've found it!

SENTENCE COMBINING:

5. The ice cream cone was introduced at the St. Louis World's Fair. This happened in 1904.

_____

_____

DAY 29

CAPITALIZATION:

1. carlos and his dog, gumdrop, went to seven lakes state park.

PUNCTUATION:

Place a period after most abbreviations. Do not use a period after the title, *Miss*, or after metric measurements.
   Examples: Miss Homer
               centimeter = cm

Write the abbreviation:

2. A. Doctor - _____   C. pound - _____   E. Drive - _____

   B. cup - _____   D. Company - _____   F. meter - _____

PARTS OF SPEECH: NOUNS
Plural means more than one.
Nouns ending in sh and ch add es to form the plural.

Write the plural:

3. A. crash - _____

   B. printer - _____

   C. stitch - _____

SUBJECT/VERB:

Cross out any prepositional phrases. Underline the subject once and the verb twice:

4. A man smiled at the baby.

SENTENCE COMBINING:

5. Aren rode his bike to Ted's house.
   Aren and Ted played chess.

_____

_____

DAY 30

CAPITALIZATION:

1. did you know that texas falls is really in the state of vermont?

PUNCTUATION:

Use a colon to set off lists.

    Examples: Art supplies:
        ~ brushes
        ~ pens
        ~ paints

    We need the following art supplies: brushes, pens, and paints.

2. Picnic items
    ~ hot dogs
    ~ buns
    ~ chips

DIFFICULT WORDS:
Circle the correct word:

3. A. I want to go (there, their, they're) with you.
   B. Did (you're, your) backpack break?

PARTS OF SPEECH: VERBS

Sometimes, a verb such as *have* will serve as a main verb.
    Example: I <u>have</u> an idea.

At other times, *have* is used with another verb and becomes a helping verb. This is called a verb phrase.
    Example: I <u>have lost</u> my dime.   (verb phrase = have lost)

Write <u>MV</u> if the boldfaced verb stands alone as a main verb; write <u>HV</u> if the boldfaced verb serves as a helping verb:

4. A. _____ Alli **has** a new kitten.
   B. _____ Mom **has gone** to get groceries.

SENTENCE COMBINING:

5. The toy was lying on the floor.
   Dad tripped over it.

_____

_____

DAY 31

CAPITALIZATION:
Do not capitalize seasons of the year.
  Examples: spring   autumn

1. last summer they went to india, a country in asia*.
*name of a continent

PUNCTUATION:
Use a comma to make a sentence clear.
  Example: In the meadow, larks chirped happily.

2. During the storm clouds rolled in

PARTS OF SPEECH: VERBS
Tense means time. The present tense expresses time now.
  Examples: Tate **rides** a motorcycle.
              Molly and Tami **ride** motorcycles.
The past tense expresses time that has already happened.
  Example: Molly and Tami **rode** motorcycles yesterday.

Place a √ if the verb expresses present time (present tense):

3. A. ___ I **am** in a play.
   B. ___ Dad **made** pickled eggs.

SYNONYMS/ANTONYMS/HOMONYMS:
Antonyms are words with opposite meanings.   Example: still - moving
Circle the antonym of the boldfaced word:

4. **departure:** a) exit   b) withdrawal   c) arrival

SENTENCE COMBINING:

5. The dentist examined Fay's teeth.
   Fay had no cavities.

_____

_____

DAY 32

CAPITALIZATION:

Capitalize the name of a special event.

 Examples: Kentucky Derby
      Loom Arts and Crafts Show
      Pine Carnival

1. the ohio senior olympics were held at peck park.

PUNCTUATION:

Place a comma between a city and a country.

 Example: London, England

2. Did seventy five people board the plane for Paris France

PARTS OF SPEECH: CONJUNCTIONS

Circle any conjunctions:

3. Lars and Anna are tired, but they need to finish the sanding.

SUBJECT/VERB:

Cross out prepositional phrases; underline the subject once and the verb twice:

4. The scuba diver arrived in a yellow car.

SENTENCE COMBINING:

5. A kitten crawled on Tom's lap.
 The kitten was soft.
 The kitten was gray.

_____

_____

DAY 33

CAPITALIZATION:

Capitalize the name of a language.

Example: Spanish

1. does mayor dink speak french with his grandmother?

PUNCTUATION:

2. At night time was set aside for camp games

PARTS OF SPEECH: VERBS

Tense means time.   The present tense expresses time now.

Examples: She **climbs** mountains.
I **climb** stairs.

The past tense expresses time that has already happened.

Example: The child **climbed** up on a hay wagon.

Place a √ if the verb expresses past time (past tense):

3. A. ___ Miss Lima **watched** slides of Nepal.
   B. ___ Her ferrets **hide** under the bed.

PARTS OF SPEECH: ADJECTIVES

Circle any special adjectives called articles:

4. Annie bought a cup at an outdoor fair.

SENTENCE COMBINING:

5. The girls washed the car.
   The girls had fun.

_____

_____

DAY 34

CAPITALIZATION:

Capitalize the first word of each line of poetry.

Example: Fog has rolled in.
Ships do not move.

Capitalize these lines of poetry:

1. a centipede was happy quite,

   until a frog in fun,

PUNCTUATION:

2. Pam add one third cup of water to that soup

PARTS OF SPEECH: NOUNS

Plural means more than one. Words ending in <u>sh</u>, <u>ch</u>, <u>x</u>, <u>z</u>, and <u>s</u> usually add <u>es</u> to form the plural.

Place a <u>√</u> if the plural of the noun is formed by adding <u>es</u>:

3. A. _____ splotch   C. _____ job   E. _____ splash
    B. _____ mix   D. _____ pillow   F. _____ bottle

PARTS OF SPEECH: ADJECTIVES

Circle any adjectives that tell <u>how many</u>:

4. A few squirrels gathered twenty nuts.

SENTENCE COMBINING:

5. Mary Joseph Hale was an author.
   She wrote "Mary Had a Little Lamb."

   _____

   _____

DAY 35

CAPITALIZATION:

Capitalize someone or something from another country. Usually part of the name of the country is used.

Example: Germany - German

1. did the japanese tourists take a boat down the tippah river?

PUNCTUATION:

Punctuate this part of a friendly letter:

2. Dear Nick

    We went fishing boating and hiking at a lake

    　　　　　　　Your aunt
    　　　　　　　Ama

PARTS OF SPEECH: VERBS

Underline the subject once. Place two lines under the verb that agrees with the subject:

3. This magazine (have, has) a page torn out.

PARTS OF SPEECH: PRONOUNS

Circle the correct answer:

4. (Me and Darin, Darin and I) are finished.

SENTENCE COMBINING:

5. The fans cheered.
   They were watching a baseball game.

_____

_____

DAY 36

CAPITALIZATION:

1. a camper at bee rock campground was taken to mercy hospital.

PUNCTUATION:

Use a hyphen to combine some closely related words.
Example: tri-level

2. Yes I ve made a three layer cake

PARTS OF SPEECH: PREPOSITIONS

A prepositional phrase begins with a preposition and ends with a noun or pronoun. That word is called an object of the preposition.

Circle any prepositional phrases; box any object(s) of the preposition:

3. They'll leave by noon on Friday.

PARTS OF SPEECH: VERBS

There are 23 helping verbs.

Add vowels to form helping verbs:

4.   d_   h_s   m_y   sh__ld   sh_ll   _s   w_s   b__ng
    d__s   h_v_   m_ght   c__ld   w_ll   _m   w_r_   b__n
    d_d   h_d   m_st   w__ld   c_n   _r_   b_

SENTENCE COMBINING:

5. An ant crawled across the sidewalk.
The ant was carrying a piece of bread.

_____

_____

DAY 37

CAPITALIZATION:

Do not capitalize plants or animals.

1. a collie is for sale at pet palace* on west king street.

* name of store

PUNCTUATION:

2. They moved to 2 Peat Street Plano Texas

SENTENCE TYPES:

A declarative sentence makes a statement.
An imperative sentence gives a command.
An interrogative sentence asks a question.
An exclamatory sentence shows excitement.

Write the type of sentence:

3. A. Sit down. _____

   B. This ribbon is loose. _____

PARTS OF SPEECH: PRONOUNS

Pronouns take the place of nouns.

Circle the correct pronoun:

4. A rooster chased _____ (I, me).

SENTENCE COMBINING:

5. A carnival will be held soon.
   A carnival will be held to raise money for the fire department.

   _____

   _____

DAY 38

CAPITALIZATION:

1. a chinese nurse will go with the birk family to union beach.

PUNCTUATION:

Use a hyphen when dividing a word of two or more syllables at the end of a line. You must have at least two letters on the first line and three letters on the next line.

Example: _____ ab-
sent _____

Divide these words at the end of a line:

2. A. butter: _____   B. replay: _____

   _____   _____

PARTS OF SPEECH: NOUNS
Capitalize any proper nouns:

3. A. gulf of mexico   C. lake   E. mississippi river
   B. river   D. lake erie   F. street

PARTS OF SPEECH: ADJECTIVES
Circle any adjectives that tell <u>what kind</u>:

4. A striped fish swam in the blue cool water.

SENTENCE COMBINING:

5. The boys ran a race.
   Dave won.

   _____

   _____

DAY 39

CAPITALIZATION:

1. kyla attends mand middle school near the atlantic ocean.

PUNCTUATION:

Punctuate this heading:

2.
                                                                                34 Lake Ave
                                                                                Tucson Arizona   85705
                                                                                January 23 20--

PARTS OF SPEECH: VERBS

Write the contraction:

3. A. do not - _____   C. they are - _____   E. I have - _____

    B. I will - _____   D. has not - _____   F. she will - _____

PARTS OF SPEECH: VERBS
Tense means time.
Present tense means now.
Past tense means something has already happened.

Write PR for present tense and PA for past tense:

4. A. ___   Lani **sleeps** in a bunk bed.
    B. ___   The campers **sang** around the fire.

SENTENCE COMBINING:

5. The small child cried.
    The small child had an ear infection.

_____

_____

DAY 40

CAPITALIZATION:

1. one ruler of england was queen victoria.

PUNCTUATION:

Use quotation marks (" ") in a direct quotation. This is exactly what someone says, and it tells the person who said it. If the person making the statement is given first, place a comma after the person's name. Place end punctuation inside the quotation marks.

      Example: Troy said, "Let's move."

2. Janet said   Take this with you

PARTS OF SPEECH: ADVERBS

Circle any adverbs that tell <u>when</u> or <u>where</u>:

3. Never go outside without permission.

DIFFICULT WORDS:

<u>Two</u> is a number.   Example: They were gone two days.
<u>Too</u> means also or overly.   Example: I ate too much, too.
<u>To</u> is a preposition.   Example: Go to bed.

Circle the correct word:

4. Your report is (to, too, two) short.

SENTENCE COMBINING:

5. Nani is reading a book.
   The book has large pictures.
   The pictures are colorful.

_____

_____

DAY 41

CAPITALIZATION:

Capitalize the name of a church, synagogue, or temple.
Examples: Temple Beth Ami
Hillside Chapel

1. did pastor sells preach at st. james lutheran church?

PUNCTUATION:

2. Millie asked   When is the party

PARTS OF SPEECH: NOUNS

A noun names a person, a place, or a thing.
Concrete nouns usually can be seen: table, tool, train
Abstract nouns usually cannot be seen: love, mercy, sadness

Place a √ if the noun is concrete:

3. A. ___ stone   C. ___ happiness   E. ___ joy
   B. ___ fear   D. ___ mansion   F. ___ porch

PARTS OF SPEECH: ADVERBS

Circle any adverbs that tell <u>how</u>:

4. He quietly gave the answer.

SENTENCE COMBINING:

5. The puppy is frisky.
   The puppy is chasing a ball.

_____

_____

DAY 42

CAPITALIZATION:

1. a. t. arkin flew to chicago last december.

PUNCTUATION:

2. No Mikes parents didnt go to Naco Mexico

PARTS OF SPEECH: NOUNS
   Write the plural:

3. A. flash - _____   D. tax - _____

   B. class - _____   E. bush - _____

   C. envelope - _____ F. layer - _____

SYNONYMS/ANTONYMS/HOMONYMS:

Synonyms are words with similar meanings.
Antonyms are words with opposite meanings.
Homonyms are words that sound alike but are spelled differently.

4. Write a homonym for lone: _____

SENTENCE COMBINING:

5. The child sneezed.
   The child coughed.
   The child took a tissue from the box.

   _____

   _____

DAY 43

CAPITALIZATION:

Remember:
Capitalize the name of a special event.

1. the eagle arts show will begin on wednesday, march 5.

PUNCTUATION:

2. Lets meet at 2 00 on Thursday February 19

PARTS OF SPEECH: ADJECTIVES
Circle any adjectives that tell which one(s):

3. Is this pencil darker than that pen?

PARTS OF SPEECH: VERBS
There are 23 helping verbs.
Add consonants to form these nine helping verbs:

4. A. the 3 *d's:*   _o   _oe_   _i_
    B. the 3 *h's:*   _a_e   _a_   _a_
    C. the *3 m's:*   _a_   _i___   _u__

SENTENCE COMBINING:

5. The car is painted red.
   The car has a flat tire.

_____

_____

DAY 44

CAPITALIZATION:

Capitalize the name of a club or organization.

Examples: American Red Cross
           Mothers of Twins Club

1. a meeting of the gleeful gardeners' club was held at ingle inn.

PUNCTUATION:

Do not place more than one period at the end of a sentence.

Example: I live on Cobweb St.

2. Her name was listed as Bane Penny S

PARTS OF SPEECH: VERBS

Add consonants to complete these helping verbs:

3. _ _ou_ _   _ _a_ _   i_   _a_   _ei_ _
   _ou_ _   _i_ _   a_   _e_e   _ee_
   _ou_ _   _a_   _r_   _e

PARTS OF SPEECH: ADJECTIVES

Circle any adjectives that tell <u>how many</u>:

4. A few boys brought only one friend to the game.

SENTENCE COMBINING:

5. Mary writes letters.
   Mary writes to her aunt.
   Mary also writes letters to her cousin.

_____

_____

DAY 45

CAPITALIZATION:

1. dear mr. flan,

    your poem entitled "the bear and the bee" is good.

    sincerely yours,

    meg lewis

PUNCTUATION:

2. The clown said Im making balloon animals

PARTS OF SPEECH: NOUNS

A common noun names any person, place, or thing.   Example: bug

A type is still a common noun.   Example: ant

A proper noun is specific. A proper noun is capitalized.
Example: common - person
proper - Anita

Write a proper noun for each common noun:

3. A. park - _____

    B. city - _____

    C. country - _____

PARTS OF SPEECH: VERBS

Underline the subject once; place two lines under the verb that agrees with the subject:

4. Luke often (swim, swims) for a few hours.

SENTENCE COMBINING:

5. My candy bar was left in the sun.
    My candy bar melted.

    _____

    _____

DAY 46

CAPITALIZATION:

1. micah and i live south of topaz tile company on zig avenue.

PUNCTUATION:

2. They ate pizza drank cola and played ball

SUBJECT/VERB:

A prepositional phrase begins with a preposition and ends with a noun or pronoun. Example: They live **in the South**.
A prepositional phrase usually won't contain a subject or verb. Cross it out. Example: They live in the South.

Cross out any prepositional phrases. Underline the subject once and the verb twice:

3. Holly works for a printing company.

PARTS OF SPEECH: ADJECTIVES

Circle any adjectives that tell which one(s):

4. Those twins look alike.

SENTENCE COMBINING:

5. Tracey's sneakers were under the bed.
   Tracey couldn't find them.

_____

_____

DAY 47

CAPITALIZATION:

1. did you see elk at yosemite national park in the spring?

PUNCTUATION:

2. The R J Lincoln Co opened last Thursday Nov 29

ALPHABETIZING:
   Write these words in alphabetical order:

3. fin   heat   grab   finish   inning   eating

   (a) _____   (d) _____
   (b) _____   (e) _____
   (c) _____   (f) _____

PARTS OF SPEECH: ADJECTIVES
   Circle any descriptive adjectives:

4. Tall weeds grew under a wilted tree.

SENTENCE COMBINING:

5. My uncle teaches art.
   My uncle teaches at a junior high.
   My uncle's name is Phil.

   _____

   _____

DAY 48

CAPITALIZATION:

1. many americans fly flags on veteran's day.

PUNCTUATION:

2. Tina did you add one fourth cup of oil to these brownies

PREFIXES/ROOTS/SUFFIXES:

A root is any "word" without a part added at the beginning or end.

Examples: statement = **state** + ment   rewrite = re + **write**
                              (root)   (suffix)   (prefix)   (root)

3. The root of **preview** is _____.

PARTS OF SPEECH: ADVERBS

Circle any adverbs that tell <u>when</u>:

4. Will you be leaving tonight or tomorrow?

SENTENCE COMBINING:

5. In 1850, settlers moved to Michigan.
   They also moved to Wisconsin.
   They also moved to southeastern Iowa.

   _____

   _____

DAY 49

CAPITALIZATION:

Capitalize the name of a museum, mansion, lighthouse, or other well-known building.
  Example: Vanderbilt Mansion

1. their friends went to glenrok art museum last friday.

PUNCTUATION:

2. Dad wheres Sen Blatz going

PARTS OF SPEECH: VERBS

Underline the subject once; place two lines under the verb that agrees with the subject:

3. The clown also (sing, sings) in his act.

PARTS OF SPEECH: NOUNS

Nouns ending in consonant + y change the y to i and add es to form the plural.   Example: buggy = buggies

Nouns ending in vowel + y just add s.
  Example: play = plays

Write the plural:

4. A. puppy - _____
    B. ray - _____
    C. monkey - _____
    D. lobby - _____

SENTENCE COMBINING:

5. Rob threw the ball.
   Sally caught the ball.

_____

_____

DAY 50

CAPITALIZATION:

1. is the statue of liberty in new york city located on liberty island?

PUNCTUATION:

Underline the title of books, magazines, and movies.

Place the title of stories, poems, reports, and articles in quotation marks (" ").

Punctuate these titles:

2. A. (book)   Moby Dick
   B. (story)   Millie
   C. (poem)   If
   D. (magazine) Baby and Mom

PARTS OF SPEECH: VERBS

Circle the correct word:

3. The winners (doesn't, don't) get a trophy.

PARTS OF SPEECH: NOUNS

A noun may show ownership. Add apostrophe (') + s to a singular (one) noun.

Example: groceries purchased by my mother: my mother's groceries

Write the possessive:

4. a map belonging to Emma - _____

SENTENCE COMBINING:

5. Chessa collects stickers.
   Chessa collects stamps.
   Chessa also collects shells.

   _____

   _____

DAY 51

CAPITALIZATION:

Remember:

Capitalize the Roman numerals (I, II, III, IV, V, etc.) and letters for each major division in an outline. Capitalize the first word of each line.

Capitalize the outline:

1. i. schools
      a. public schools
      b. private schools

PUNCTUATION:

2. I need the following vegetables carrots potatoes and onions

PARTS OF SPEECH: ADVERBS

Circle any adverbs that tell <u>where</u>:

3. Has everyone gone inside?

PARTS OF SPEECH: VERBS

Some verbs show action.
Some verbs make a statement.

Place a √ if the verb shows action:

4. A. ___ Laura <u>glued</u> felt to a paper.
   B. ___ Matt and Molly <u>placed</u> screens on their windows.
   C. ___ You <u>seem</u> sad.

SENTENCE COMBINING:

5. Sally's lock was broken.
   Sally bought a new one.

_____

_____

DAY 52

CAPITALIZATION:

1. little brad has read the book, here comes the snow.

PUNCTUATION:
   Punctuate this heading and greeting (salutation) of a friendly letter:

2.   52 Elm Ln
                                                                   Gettysburg PA   17325
                                                                   May 8 20--

   Dear Paco

PARTS OF SPEECH: NOUNS
   Place a √ if the noun is common:

3. A. ___ Jane   D. ___ Thorn Theater
    B. ___ poodle   E. ___ school
    C. ___ New Mexico   F. ___ market

PARTS OF SPEECH: VERBS
   Underline the subject once. Place two lines under the verb that agrees with the subject:

4. My cousins (visits, visit) often.

SENTENCE COMBINING:

5. We watched television.
    We ate popcorn.

_____

_____

DAY 53

CAPITALIZATION:

Do not capitalize a school subject unless it's a language or has a number.

        Examples: science
                                Art I
                                Spanish

1. last fall, mrs. kirk's reading class went to a library on elton circle.

PUNCTUATION:

2.   I   Arizona
       A Climate
       B Cities

PARTS OF SPEECH: VERBS

    <u>Can</u> **means to be able to.**
    <u>May</u> **states a possibility or asks permission.**

Circle the correct verb:

3. I (may, can) have to wait until Friday.

PARTS OF SPEECH: CONJUNCTIONS/INTERJECTIONS

Circle any conjunctions; box any interjections:

4. Whoa! Slow down or stop!

SENTENCE COMBINING:

5. The man drew a picture.
   The man is an artist.
   The picture was of a clown.

_____

_____

DAY 54

CAPITALIZATION:
   Capitalize both letters of a state postal code.   Example: Utah - UT
Capitalize this heading and greeting:

1.   333 strom street
                                                                   shippensburg, pa   17257
                                                                   april 22, 20--

   dear yancy,

PUNCTUATION:

2.   No Katies pen wont work

PARTS OF SPEECH: ADJECTIVES
   Circle any articles and descriptive adjectives:

3.   A white furry bunny hopped to me.

DIFFICULT WORDS:
   Circle the correct word:

4.   A.   (Their, They're, There) teacher is absent.
     B.   I think that (it's, its) paw is stuck.

SENTENCE COMBINING:

5.   The dessert is delicious.
     The dessert is pie.
     The pie is apple.

   _____

   _____

DAY 55

CAPITALIZATION:

Capitalize the first word of a direct quotation. A direct quotation states what a person has said.

Example: Liz asked, "What are you doing?"

1. maria said, "ted and i will come on friday."

PUNCTUATION:

Remember:

Underline the title of books, magazines, and movies.
Place the title of stories, poems, reports, and articles in quotation marks (" ").

Punctuate these titles:

2. A. (report)   Mars
   B. (movie)   Summer of the Monkeys

PARTS OF SPEECH: PREPOSITIONS

Circle any prepositional phrases:

3. The rug in the middle of the room is from China.

PARTS OF SPEECH: VERBS

Tense means time.
Present tense means now.
Past tense means something has already happened.

Write **PR** for present tense and **PA** for past tense:

4. A. ___ The woman **welded** some metal.
   B. ___ He **draws** cartoons.

SENTENCE COMBINING:

5. The test was difficult.
   The test was about fractions.

_____

_____

DAY 56

CAPITALIZATION:

1. miss dixon asked, "is the south mountain fair held in september?"

PUNCTUATION:

2. Send the box to 1 York Avenue St Paul Minnesota 55101

DIFFICULT WORDS:

Circle the correct word:

3. A. We heard that (you're, your) essay won a prize.
   B. He answered (to, two, too) questions.

PARTS OF SPEECH: NOUNS

Plural means more than one.
Some words do not change to form the plural:

Example: one sheep - two sheep

Write the plural:

4. A. box - _____
   B. brush - _____
   C. spray - _____
   D. deer - _____
   E. secretary - _____

SENTENCE COMBINING:

5. Jana was angry.
   Jana left the room.

   _____

   _____

DAY 57

CAPITALIZATION:
Capitalize Mom, Dad, and other titles if you can insert the person's name.
Example: I'm sure that you are right, **M**om.

1. did dad ever live on east elm lane in lubbock, texas?

PUNCTUATION:

2. Jana asked Are we leaving at 2 15 today

PREFIXES/ROOTS/SUFFIXES:
A prefix is attached to a root at the beginning of a word.
Prefixes have meanings: un, non, il, im = not
Example: illegal = not legal

3. A. What is the prefix of impolite? _____

   B. What does impolite mean? _____

SENTENCE TYPES:
A declarative sentence makes a statement.
An imperative sentence is a command.
An interrogative sentence asks a question.
An exclamatory sentence shows excitement or strong emotion.

Write the type of sentence:

4. A. No! I'm stranded!   _____

   B. May I help you?   _____

SENTENCE COMBINING:

5. The owl sat in a tree.
   The owl hooted.

_____

_____

DAY 58

CAPITALIZATION:

Capitalize the brand name but not the product.
Example: Delite ham

1. roy exclaimed, "this goody* glue is great!"

*brand name

PUNCTUATION:

2. Max exclaimed   Yikes   We are lost

PARTS OF SPEECH: ADJECTIVES
Circle any adjectives telling how many:

3. Several children played together.

FRIENDLY LETTERS:
A friendly letter contains five parts:

                                  44 Elm Street
                HEADING   Phoenix, Arizona   85013
                                  April 1, 20--

GREETING   Dear Ryan,   *(or SALUTATION)*

BODY   Hi! My friends and I will meet you in Detroit next week.

                           CLOSING   Your friend,
                        SIGNATURE Collin

4.   A. What is on the first line of a heading? _____

      B. What is *Dear Ryan* called? _____

SENTENCE COMBINING:

5. Gloria was shouting for her brother.
   Gloria became hoarse.

_____

_____

DAY 59

CAPITALIZATION:

Capitalize the first word of each line of poetry.

Capitalize these lines of a poem entitled "If Ever I See":

1. i must not in play,

   steal the birds away,

PUNCTUATION:

Write the abbreviation:

2. A. Elk Mountain - Elk_____ C. quart - _____ E. yard - _____

   B. United States - _____ D. meter - _____ F. Lane - _____

PARTS OF SPEECH: NOUNS

A noun may show ownership. Add apostrophe (') + s to a singular (one) noun to show possession.

Write the possessive form:

3. a balloon belonging to a child - _____

SUBJECT/VERB:

There may be two or more subjects in a sentence. This is called a compound subject.
   Example: A <u>rabbit</u>, a <u>deer</u>, and a tiny <u>mouse</u> <u>were</u> <s>in the garden</s>.

Underline the subject once; place two lines under the verb:

4. Joey and his dad laugh frequently.

SENTENCE COMBINING:

5. The post card is from our cousin.
   The post card is torn.
   It has a picture of a beach on the front.

   _____

   _____

DAY 60

CAPITALIZATION:

1. have mr. montoya and dr. jones played tennis at the top seed club?

PUNCTUATION:

2. Theyve read twenty seven pages of How to Eat Fried Worms*

*title of a book

SUBJECT/VERB:

   Underline the subject once and the verb twice:

3. Andrew and I fished yesterday.

PARTS OF SPEECH: VERBS

   Write an appropriate helping verb (or verbs) in each blank:

   Example: The dog _____has_____ barked.
   The dog ___should have___ barked.

4. A. He _____ go with you.

   He _____ go with you.

   B. They _____ swinging.

   They _____ swinging.

SENTENCE COMBINING:

5. The road is dirt.
   The road has many loose stones.
   The road is bumpy.

   _____

   _____

DAY 61

CAPITALIZATION:

1. they visited old mission lighthouse on the atlantic ocean.

PUNCTUATION:

2. During the hurricane wind was strong and gusty

PARTS OF SPEECH: VERBS
Write the contraction:

3. A. have not - _____

   B. you are - _____

   C. he will - _____

   D. they have - _____

   E. I am - _____

PARTS OF SPEECH: ADJECTIVES
Circle any adjectives that tell which one(s):

4. These rods seem good, but I'll take that net.

SENTENCE COMBINING:

5. The Spanish learned to make tamales.
   They learned to make them from the Aztec Indians.

   _____

   _____

DAY 62

CAPITALIZATION:

1. their alaskan guests stayed at the blue moose lodge.

PUNCTUATION:

2. Carrie exclaimed Look at that boat

PARTS OF SPEECH: NOUNS
   Write the plural:

3. A. boy - _____

   B. crash - _____

   C. buzz - _____

   D. field - _____

   E. baby - _____

SUBJECT/VERB:
   Cross out any prepositional phrases. Underline the subject once and the verb twice.

4. They soaked in a campground hot tub.

SENTENCE COMBINING:

5. Mom made sandwiches.
   Dad made a salad.
   The food was for lunch.

   _____

   _____

DAY 63

CAPITALIZATION:

Do not capitalize foods.
Example: We ate a bacon, lettuce, and tomato sandwich.

1. the kline family ate steak and eggs at cactus cafe in hoover mall.

PUNCTUATION:

If a noun is plural *and* ends in s, place an apostrophe after the s to show ownership.
Example: A teachers' meeting was held after school.

2. Mrs Trueblood attended a popular songwriters conference in a large California city

PARTS OF SPEECH: PRONOUNS
Circle the correct pronoun:

3. Jill and _____ (I, me) were selected.

PARTS OF SPEECH: ADJECTIVES
Circle any adjectives that tell what kind:

4. Lynn's blue shirt matches your plaid skirt.

SENTENCE COMBINING:

5. Juice was served first.
   It was orange juice.
   Milk was served later.

_____

_____

DAY 64

CAPITALIZATION:

1. ms. tang stayed near florida bay in dade county.

PUNCTUATION:

2. Place my name in the telephone book as Ross T M

PARTS OF SPEECH: NOUNS

A noun names a person, a place, or a thing.
Concrete nouns usually can be seen: harp, countertop, tractor
Abstract nouns usually cannot be seen: joy, fear

Place a √ if the noun is concrete:

3. A. ___ delight   C. ___ shed   E. ___ salt
    B. ___ cloud   D. ___ misery   F. ___ care

SYNONYMS/ANTONYMS/HOMONYMS:

Synonyms are words with similar meanings.
Antonyms are words with opposite meanings.
Homonyms are words that sound alike but are spelled differently.

4. A. Write a synonym for *answer*: _____

    B. Write an antonym for *final*: _____

SENTENCE COMBINING:

5. Jack runs fast.
    Annie runs faster.

    _____

    _____

DAY 65

CAPITALIZATION:

Capitalize the first word of a direct quotation.

Example: Anna said, "I'm leaving."

If the person talking appears after the spoken words, do not capitalize the word *said* or similar word.

Example: "I'm leaving," said Anna.

1. "have you been to sedge island?" asked ron.

PUNCTUATION:

Punctuate this part of a friendly letter:

2. Dear Alicia

   Youre staying with us next summer

           Love
           Jenny

PARTS OF SPEECH: ADJECTIVES

Circle any adjectives that tell which one(s):

3. Did you paint this picture?

PARTS OF SPEECH: VERBS

Sometimes a sentence contains two or more verbs. This is called a compound verb.

Example: The baker whipped some cream and put it aside.

Underline the subject once and the verb twice:

4. I chopped onions and fried them.

SENTENCE COMBINING:

5. Randy had a party.
   It was a birthday party.
   Fifteen friends attended.

_____

_____

DAY 66

CAPITALIZATION:

Remember:
Do not capitalize foods, games, plants, or animals.

1. our neighbor buys potato chips at franco food factory on deer lane.

PUNCTUATION:

2. Hasnt that chests hinge been fixed

PARTS OF SPEECH: VERBS

Write the 23 helping (auxiliary) verbs:

3. d_____ h_____ m_____ sh_____ sh_____ i_____ w_____ b_____
   d_____ h_____ m_____ c_____   w_____   a_____ w_____ b_____
   d_____ h_____ m_____ w_____   c_____   a_____ b_____

PARTS OF SPEECH:

Circle the correct word:

4. (Their, There, They're) uncle likes to ski.

SENTENCE COMBINING:

5. The day was cold.
   The day was windy.
   The day was sunny.

_____

_____

DAY 67

CAPITALIZATION:

1. on independence day, grandpa meese planted roses along briar alley.

PUNCTUATION:

2. Theyll be leaving for Madrid* Spain

*name of a city

PARTS OF SPEECH: VERBS

Some verbs can serve as a helping verb or as a main verb.

    Examples: I <u>am</u> a student.   (main verb)

                     I <u>am going</u> to meet my friend. (helping verb)

3. A. Write a sentence using *has* as a main verb:

   _____

   B. Write a sentence using *has* as a helping verb:

   _____

PARTS OF SPEECH: ADVERBS

Circle any adverbs that tell <u>how</u>:

4. The salesman wrote slowly and carefully.

SENTENCE COMBINING:

5. The floor is wet.
   Cameron has spilled lemonade.

   _____

   _____

DAY 68

CAPITALIZATION:

1. their group saw <u>the king and i</u> at ramos theater.

PUNCTUATION:
Use underlining or quotation marks:

2. A. (book)   Tex
   B. (story)   Cat and the Underworld
   C. (magazine)   Friends and Family

PARTS OF SPEECH: PRONOUNS
Pronouns take the place of nouns.
Circle the correct pronoun:

3. That woman loves to travel.

   _____ (She, Her) loves to travel.

PARTS OF SPEECH: ADVERBS
Circle any adverbs that tell <u>when</u>:

4. Now and then, we stop for a rest.

SENTENCE COMBINING:

5. Her hair is brown.
   Her hair is curly.
   Her hair needs to be combed.

   _____

   _____

DAY 69

CAPITALIZATION:

Remember:

Capitalize the name of a club or organization.

1. the aztec riding club raised money for the bradford county rodeo.

PUNCTUATION:

Place end punctuation:

2. A. Are you leaving
   B. Please leave
   C. I'm leaving
   D. Yeah! We're leaving

FRIENDLY LETTER:

The parts of a friendly letter are body, greeting, closing, heading, and signature.

Label the parts of this friendly letter:

3.
```
                    (A)_____    22 Doe Lane
                                     Ogden, UT  84415
                                     May 9, 20--
     Dear Anya,    (B)_____
           We are having a great time here in Portland.  (C)_____
                                     Love,   (D)_____
                                     Dana    (E)_____
```

PREFIXES/ROOTS/SUFFIXES:

4. The root of **improper** is _____.

SENTENCE COMBINING:

5. The fair will be held next week.
   It is a state fair.
   We are going.

_____

_____

DAY 70

CAPITALIZATION:

Remember:

Capitalize a museum, mansion, or other well-known place.

1. "was george washington's home called mount vernon?" asked tina.

PUNCTUATION:

2. Sally asked   Wheres Mikes new boat

PARTS OF SPEECH: ADJECTIVES

Circle any adjectives that tell <u>how many</u>:

3. A few squirrels gathered twenty nuts.

PARTS OF SPEECH:

Do not use two negative words in the same sentence.
Negative words include *no, not (n't), nobody, none,* and *nothing.*

Circle the correct word:

4. He doesn't remember (nothing, anything) about the incident.

SENTENCE COMBINING:

5. Mrs. Lu is a pilot.
   Mrs. Lu owns an airplane.

   _____

   _____

DAY 71

CAPITALIZATION:

Capitalize this friendly letter:

1.
                                                      763 east park avenue

                                                      salem, nc   27108

                                                      february 12, 20--

dear mario,

       we traveled through the great salt lake desert to get to sugar canyon.

                                                      your pen pal,

                                                      pippa

PUNCTUATION:

2.   May I join a girls bowling team that plays at 6 00 on Thursdays

PARTS OF SPEECH: **VERBS**

A verb phrase is made up of a helping verb (or helping verbs) plus a main verb.

        Examples: Her cousin <u>should have taken</u> a bus.

                            I <u>must tie</u> my shoe.

Place two lines under the verb phrase:

3.   We have spent our last dollar.

PARTS OF SPEECH: **NOUNS**

Capitalize any proper noun:

4.   A. garnet corporation   D. fido

     B. mummy mountain   E. springer spaniel   (breed of dog)

     C. newspaper

SENTENCE COMBINING:

5.   A raccoon has a furry body.
     It has a long tail.
     It has black rings on its tail.

_____

_____

DAY 72

CAPITALIZATION:

1. does aunt bea attend jewish allied temple?

PUNCTUATION:

Underline the title of books, magazines, newspapers, and movies. Place the title of stories, poems, reports, and articles in quotation marks (" ").

Punctuate these titles:

2. A. (newspaper)   The Star Tribune

   B. (newspaper article)   Storm Hits Area

PARTS OF SPEECH: NOUNS

Write the plural form:

3. A. holiday - _____

   B. study - _____

   C. dish - _____

   D. melon - _____

PARTS OF SPEECH: VERBS

Place two lines under the correct verb:

4. Please (set, sit) down.

SENTENCE COMBINING:

5. The lake is very deep.
   The lake is called Crater Lake.
   The lake is in Oregon.

_____

_____

DAY 73

CAPITALIZATION:

1. he began working as a salesman for reems auto center on monday.

PUNCTUATION:

2. Tami asked Have you read The Staircase*

*book title

PARTS OF SPEECH: PRONOUNS
Circle the correct pronoun:

3. May Tito and _____ (I, me) go to the library?

ALPHABETIZING:
Write these words in alphabetical order:

4. mist   nasty   mine   opal   netting   main

(a) _____   (d) _____
(b) _____   (e) _____
(c) _____   (f) _____

SENTENCE COMBINING:

5. That shop sells flowers.
   That shop opened last week.
   I bought some daisies.

_____

_____

DAY 74

CAPITALIZATION:

1. our friend from austria arrived at richmond international airport.

PUNCTUATION:

2. Good grief Weve added one fourth cup too much vinegar

PARTS OF SPEECH: ADVERBS
   Circle any adverbs that tell <u>where</u>:

3. The teacher looked up and wrote something down.

PARTS OF SPEECH: VERBS
   Remember: verb phrase = helping verb(s) + main verb
Underline the subject once and the verb phrase twice:

4. They have (went, gone) home.

SENTENCE COMBINING:

5. The vase was a ceramic one.
   The vase was pink.
   The vase was filled with straw.

_____

_____

DAY 75

CAPITALIZATION:

1. we went to clear springs for a picnic on memorial day.

PUNCTUATION:

2. Kim said My brother is twenty one years old

PARTS OF SPEECH: NOUNS
   Place a √ if the noun is proper:

3. A. _____ steak   D. _____ Yankee Stadium

   B. _____ Hilldale Bank   E. _____ shepherd

   C. _____ Redfield Road

PARTS OF SPEECH: VERBS
   Remember: verb phrase = helping verb(s) + main verb
   Underline the subject once and the verb phrase twice:

4. Her boss must have (gave, given) her a bonus.

SENTENCE COMBINING:

5. Joanie went ice skating.
   Her sister went, too.
   They went to Bardton Pond.

   _____

   _____

DAY 76

CAPITALIZATION:

Capitalize the name of a religion, a religious document, and the name for a supreme being.

Examples: Judaism   (religion)
           Koran   (Moslem holy book)

1. a christian festivity was held in bethlehem last spring.

PUNCTUATION:

2. Candy lets eat breakfast clean our rooms and ride our bikes

PARTS OF SPEECH: VERBS

Underline the subject once. Place two lines under the verb that agrees with the subject:

3. Her aunt (uses, use) her computer daily.

DIFFICULT WORDS:

Circle the correct word:

4. A. (Your, You're) sunglasses are on the table.

   B. (It's, Its) probably too late to go there.

   C. His brother wants to meet us, (to, two, too).

SENTENCE COMBINING:

5. Danno's lunch is in the refrigerator.
   The lunch consists of a sandwich and cookies.

_____

_____

DAY 77

CAPITALIZATION:

Capitalize the outline:

1. i. lakes
   a. fresh water
   b. salt water

PUNCTUATION:

Use quotation marks in a direct quotation. This is exactly what someone says and states the person who said it. If the person making the <u>statement</u> is placed after the quotation, place a comma inside the last quotation mark.

   Example: "Give that to me," said Ricky.

2. Youre our leader   said Artie

SENTENCE TYPES:
Write the sentence type:

3. A. That's more like it! _____
   B. Take this paper, please. _____
   C. Kino is here. _____

PARTS OF SPEECH: NOUNS

Write the possessive:

4. tires on a bus - _____

SENTENCE COMBINING:

5. This watch is new.
   This watch is blue.
   This watch was given to Barbara as a graduation gift.

   _____

   _____

DAY 78

CAPITALIZATION:

1. many youngsters ate yogurt and played tag at the burnsville children's festival.

PUNCTUATION:

> **In a direct quotation, place a question mark before the second quotation mark if the person is asking a question. Place an exclamation point if the person is showing excitement. (Usually, *said* is replaced by *exclaimed* or *shouted*.)**
>
> Example: "Did I get a part in the play?" asked Luis.
> "Follow me!" exclaimed Mrs. Dino.

2. What is a two humped camel called   asked Sharon

PARTS OF SPEECH: CONJUNCTIONS
   Circle any conjunctions:

3. My mother and I will help you, but we must eat first.

PARTS OF SPEECH: NOUNS
   Circle any nouns:

4. Adanna ate macaroni and cheese for lunch.

SENTENCE COMBINING:

5. They went fishing at a lake.
   They caught five fish.
   Mom and Dad went.

_____

_____

DAY 79

CAPITALIZATION:

1. on labor day, rabbi good and his family went to mono hot springs.

PUNCTUATION:

2. Drinks for picnic
     ~ lemonade
     ~ water
     ~ soda

PARTS OF SPEECH: ADJECTIVES

   Circle any articles (a special type of adjective):

3. A tugboat pulled up to the dock.

SUBJECT/VERB:

   There may be two or more subjects in a sentence. This is called a compound subject.
   Example: <u>Oranges</u> and <u>lemons</u> are in that bowl.

   Underline the subject once; place two lines under the verb:

4. The bride and her attendants are nervous.

SENTENCE COMBINING:

5. The bike race began.
   I fell off my bike.
   I skinned my knee.

   _____

   _____

DAY 80

CAPITALIZATION:

1. did uncle bill read the hotel herald* at the los angeles convention center?

*magazine title

PUNCTUATION:

2. Her uncles friend wants to live at 12 Main Street Meredith NH 03253

PARTS OF SPEECH: PREPOSITIONS

Remember: An object of the preposition is the noun or pronoun that ends a prepositional phrase.

Circle any prepositional phrases; box any object(s) of the preposition:

3. Rain pounded on the roof of our car.

PARTS OF SPEECH: ADVERBS

Circle any adverbs that tell how:

4. Mary kissed the child lovingly.

SENTENCE COMBINING:

5. The first Russian settlement in America was started in 1809.
   It was started at Bodega Bay.

_____

_____

DAY 81

CAPITALIZATION:

1. the lady said, "i bought a twirly* race car for my grandson."

*brand name

PUNCTUATION:

Underline titles of books, magazines, newspapers, plays, and movies. Place quotation marks around the titles of stories, poems, songs, reports, articles, and chapters.

Punctuate these titles:

2. A. (song)   Arise and Shine
   B. (book)   Roll of Thunder, Hear My Cry
   C. (poem)   On a Rainy Day

PARTS OF SPEECH: ADJECTIVES

Those is a pronoun if it stands alone.
      Example: I like those.
Those is an adjective if it modifies (goes over to) a noun.
      Example: Are those shoes too tight?   (those shoes)
Them is a pronoun. It always stands alone.

Circle the correct word:

3. Have you seen (them, those) kittens?

PARTS OF SPEECH: VERBS

Circle the correct helping verb:

4. (Can, May) he find their phone number?

SENTENCE COMBINING:

5. His shoes are blue.
   His shoes are tennis shoes.
   His shoes are in the corner of the room.

_____

_____

DAY 82

CAPITALIZATION:

Capitalize the names of historic events.
Example: Civil War

1. a german mayor visited fort collins during the korean war.

PUNCTUATION:

Punctuate this outline:

2. I Cats
      A Persian
         1 History
         2 Habits
      B Siamese

SUBJECT/VERB:

Cross out any prepositional phrases. Underline the subject once and the verb twice.

3. The bus with flashing lights stopped.

PARTS OF SPEECH: INTERJECTIONS

Circle any interjections:

4. Wow! I'm really early!

SENTENCE COMBINING:

5. Tom's aunt is a teacher.
   She teaches social studies.
   She lives in Detroit.

_____

_____

DAY 83

CAPITALIZATION:

1. did officer r. b. hood go east on the garden state parkway?

PUNCTUATION:
   Write the abbreviation:

2. A. Friday - _____   C. January - _____

   B. department - _____   D. cup - _____

PARTS OF SPEECH: VERBS
   Tense means time.
   Future tense means something will happen. *Shall* and *will* are used to express future tense. Use *shall* with I.
      Example: Larry will wrap the box.

   Write P for present tense, PT for past tense, and FT for future tense:

3. A. ___ The mare **reared** on its hind legs.
   B. ___ Their grandfather **writes** poetry.
   C. ___ Your class **will begin** in August.

PARTS OF SPEECH: ADJECTIVES
   Circle any adjectives that tell what kind:

4. Cold sandwiches and chocolate cake were served.

SENTENCE COMBINING:

5. That horse is a palomino.
   That horse is named Colonel.

   _____

   _____

DAY 84

CAPITALIZATION:

Capitalize these two lines from the poem, "The Dream Ship":

1. when all the world is fast asleep,

    along the midnight skies,

PUNCTUATION:

Punctuate this friendly note:

2. Dear Alonza
       We found it fun to go to Rome Italy
    In the country people sang many beauti
    ful songs and entertained us
                        Ellen

PARTS OF SPEECH: VERBS

Remember: verb phrase = helping verb(s) + main verb
Underline the verb phrase twice:

3. The boy has (ran, run) three miles.

PARTS OF SPEECH: ADVERBS
Circle any adverbs that tell <u>how</u>:

4. A cow mooed loudly.

SENTENCE COMBINING:

5. The wagon has black tires.
   The wagon is painted green.
   The wagon has a new handle.

   _____

   _____

DAY 85

CAPITALIZATION:

1. "we are going to south america in april," said ruth.

PUNCTUATION:
   Place a comma after an interrupter at the beginning of a sentence. An interrupter is a word or phrase that isn't necessary.
   Example: *Of course*, you may go.
   interrupter

2. By the way she cuts both of my parents hair

PARTS OF SPEECH: ADJECTIVES
   Circle any adjectives that tell <u>which one(s)</u>:

3. These shoes should match that dress.

PARTS OF SPEECH: VERBS
   Sometimes a sentence contains two or more verbs. This is called a compound verb.
   Example: One worker <u>poured</u> and <u>smoothed</u> wet cement.
   Underline the subject once and the verb twice:

4. Several boys washed and dried dishes at camp.

SENTENCE COMBINING:

5. It rained all day.
   The children had to stay inside.

   _____

   _____

DAY 86

CAPITALIZATION:

1. when was the liberty bell moved to independence hall?

PUNCTUATION:

2. Dont go pleaded Peter

SUBJECT/VERB:

   Cross out any prepositional phrases. Underline the subject once and the verb twice:

3. An elk stopped by the road.

PREFIXES/ROOTS/SUFFIXES:

   A suffix is an ending. A suffix is added to a root.

   Example: resting = rest + **ing**
   　　　　　　　　　　　(root)　　(suffix)

4. The suffix of **cupful** is _____.

SENTENCE COMBINING:

5. A monkey was sitting on a tree limb.
   Another monkey was swinging on a rope.

   _____

   _____

DAY 87

CAPITALIZATION:

Capitalize these titles:

1. A. a busy year

   B. "riding the train"

   C. have you seen bugs

PUNCTUATION:

2. May I help you   asked the clerk

SENTENCE TYPES:

Write the type of sentence:

3. A. Please come here.   _____

   B. Has Jill arrived?   _____

PARTS OF SPEECH: NOUNS

Place a √ if the noun is abstract:

4. A. ____ desk
   B. ____ love
   C. ____ honesty
   D. ____ building

SENTENCE COMBINING:

5. An invitation to a wedding came in the mail.
   Gail and Gabe will be marrying.

   _____

   _____

DAY 88

CAPITALIZATION:

1. "may i go with you to new zealand?" asked miss thon.

PUNCTUATION:

2. Yes Tommys dad will arrive on Monday July 30

PARTS OF SPEECH: NOUNS
   If the noun that shows possession is plural and ends in s, place an apostrophe (') after the s.

   Example: two monkey**s'** playfulness

Write the possessive:

3. a ball belonging to two babies - _____

PARTS OF SPEECH: ADVERBS
   Circle any adverbs that tell <u>when</u>:

4. Will you be coming later?

SENTENCE COMBINING:

5. The first orange groves were planted at San Gabriel Mission.
   This mission was in California.
   They were planted around 1800.

   _____

   _____

DAY 89

CAPITALIZATION:

1. captain sees said, "my grandfather fought in world war II."

PUNCTUATION:

2. Did Cameo Dan and Erica watch a movie called Sabrina

PARTS OF SPEECH: NOUNS
If the noun that shows possession is plural and ends in s, place an apostrophe (') after the s.

        Example: two girls' lamb

Write the possessive:

3. a tent belonging to three campers - _____

PARTS OF SPEECH: ADJECTIVES
Adjectives can make comparisons.
When comparing two ONE-SYLLABLE describing words, use er.
When comparing three or more ONE-SYLLABLE describing words, use est.

    Example: soft
               softer   **(2)** This pillow is soft**er** than that one.
               softest   **(3)** Of the three, the blue pillow is soft**est**.

Circle the correct adjective:

4. That building is (taller, tallest) than this one.

SENTENCE COMBINING:

5. Jemima collects pillow cases.
   She collects antique ones.
   She collects ones with lace trim.

_____

_____

DAY 90

CAPITALIZATION:

1. christina spoke italian when she was in the peace corps*.

*name of an organization

PUNCTUATION:

2. Write your name with your last name first: _____

PARTS OF SPEECH: VERBS
   Write the contraction:

3. A. could not - _____   D. cannot - _____

   B. it is - _____   E. will not - _____

   C. I am - _____   F. what is - _____

PARTS OF SPEECH: ADVERBS
   There are seven adverbs that tell *to what extent (how much)*:
      not, so, very, too, quite, rather, somewhat

   Write an adverb telling <u>to what extent</u> that rhymes with each word:

4. A. toe - _____   D. might - _____

   B. do - _____   E. lather - _____

   C. berry - _____   F. hot - _____

SENTENCE COMBINING:

5. The woman opened the blueprint.
   She laid it on the table.
   She studied it.

   _____

   _____

DAY 91

CAPITALIZATION:

Capitalize *Native American*, *Indian*, and the name of each tribe.

Example: Did the Seneca Indian tribe live near the Hudson River?

1. the shoshone indian tribe must be proud of sacagawea*.

* famous female guide

PUNCTUATION:
Punctuate these titles:

2. A. (magazine)   Hairdos
   B. (poem)   If
   C. (newspaper) National Report

DIFFICULT WORDS:
Circle the correct word:

3. (Their, There, They're) making ice cream.

SUBJECT/VERB:

Cross out the prepositional phrase. Underline the subject once and the verb/verb phrase twice:

4. My grandpa is in that race.

SENTENCE COMBINING:

5. The necklace was made of noodles.
   Cody made it in nursery school.

_____

_____

DAY 92

CAPITALIZATION:

1. melissa said, "i saw elephants when visiting africa last november."

PUNCTUATION:
   Punctuate this friendly letter:
2.   31 Core Dr
                           (A)   Birmingham Alabama 35223
                                                 Sept 27   20--

(B)   Dear Ted
(C)   Ill be home for Thanksgiving   Will there be thirty two guests again
                                   (D)   Sincerely
                                   (E)   Bart

FRIENDLY LETTER:
   The parts of a friendly letter are body, closing, heading, signature, and greeting.

   Label the parts of the above friendly letter:

3.   A. _____   D. _____
     B. _____   E. _____
     C. _____

PREFIXES/ROOTS/SUFFIXES:

4. Write the prefix and the root of **dislike**:   prefix - _____   root - _____

SENTENCE COMBINING:

5. A daddy longlegs is also called a harvestman.
It is related to spiders.

_____

_____

DAY 93

CAPITALIZATION:

Do not capitalize foods or games. However, if a proper adjective appears with the food, capitalize the proper adjective.

Remember: **A proper adjective comes from a proper noun.**

Examples: Poland - Polish sausage
China - Chinese checkers

1. for our thanksgiving dinner, mississippi mud pie was served.

PUNCTUATION:

2. By the way those golfers tee time is 6 00

PARTS OF SPEECH: NOUNS

Some nouns totally change to form the plural.

Example: one ox - many oxen

Write the plural:

3. A. face - _____

   B. story - _____

   C. flash - _____

   D. Sunday - _____

   E. goose - _____

PARTS OF SPEECH: PRONOUNS

Circle the correct pronoun:

4. Marcy nudged _____ (me, I) and smiled.

SENTENCE COMBINING:

5. The check is on the table.
   The check is for your lunch.

_____

_____

DAY 94

CAPITALIZATION:

1. every christmas eve the rios family goes to bell mountain ski area.

PUNCTUATION:

2. Maj R Dobbs spoke about life in 1215 B C

SYNONYMS/ANTONYMS/HOMONYMS:
   Synonyms are words with similar meanings.
   Antonyms are words with opposite meanings.
   Homonyms are words that sound alike but are spelled differently.

3. A. Write a synonym for *buy*: _____

   B. Write an antonym for *buy*: _____

   C. Write a homonym for *buy*: _____

PARTS OF SPEECH:
   Do not use two negative words in the same sentence.
   Negative words include *no, not (n't), nobody, none, never,* **and** *nothing.*
   Circle the correct word:

4. He never loans (anybody, nobody) his car.

SENTENCE COMBINING:

5. The glue stick was on the floor.
   Dakota picked it up.

   _____

   _____

DAY 95

CAPITALIZATION:

1. did mayor link sail on a french liner in the pacific ocean?

PUNCTUATION:

Punctuate this closing and signature of a letter:

2. Sincerely yours
   Mario C Rubio

SENTENCE TYPES:

The types of sentences are declarative, imperative, interrogative, and exclamatory.

Write the type of sentence:

3. A. May I try that? _____

   B. Ouch! That hurt! _____

PARTS OF SPEECH: VERBS

Underline the subject once and the verb phrase twice:

4. The family had (drove, driven) many miles.

SENTENCE COMBINING:

5. Milly and Cal are riding horses.
   They are riding along a bridle path in a park.

   _____

   _____

DAY 96

CAPITALIZATION:

1. has william perry ever played football for the chicago bears*?

* name of a football team

PUNCTUATION:

2. Thats two ply bathroom tissue said Miss Goya

PARTS OF SPEECH: PREPOSITIONS

　Cross out any prepositional phrases; circle any objects of the preposition:

3. A yard sale was held on Thursday and Friday.

PARTS OF SPEECH: ADVERBS

　　Adverbs can make comparisons.
　　If two items are being compared, use <u>er</u> for ONE-SYLLABLE adverbs.
　　If three or more items are being compared, use <u>est</u> for ONE-SYLLABLE adverbs.
　　　　　　Example:　I run fast.
　　　　　　　　　　　Aren runs faster than Marco.
　　　　　　　　　　　Clark ran fastest during his third race.
　Circle the correct form:

4. Susan drew a line (straighter, straightest) than her sister.

SENTENCE COMBINING:

5. Micah went to a hardware store.
　　Before that, he went to a bookstore.

_____

_____

DAY 97

CAPITALIZATION:

1.   66421 chapel hills drive
      colorado springs, co   80920
      july 3, 20--

   dear aunt jenny,

      let's go to picadilly square in london when we are in england.

         your niece,
         tanesha

PUNCTUATION:

2.   After the snow men plowed the roads

DIFFICULT WORDS:
Circle the correct word:

3.   A.   He wants the bat if (its, it's) not broken.

   B.   Are you sure that (you're, your) next?

   C.   You hurry (to, two, too) much.

PARTS OF SPEECH: ADJECTIVES
Circle any adjectives that tell how many:

4.   One artist had many paintings in the display.

SENTENCE COMBINING:

5.   The stapler was empty.
   Sheri filled it.

_____

_____

DAY 98

CAPITALIZATION:

1. in the spring, senator cane will go to the country of chile in south america.

PUNCTUATION:

2. Susan your dog is cute friendly and frisky

PARTS OF SPEECH: NOUNS

If the noun that shows possession is plural and ends in s, place an apostrophe (') after the s.
      Example: a candy bar shared by two girls - girls' candy bar

Write the possessive:

3. a path used by many riders - _____

PARTS OF SPEECH: VERBS

Underline the subject once. Place two lines under the verb that agrees with the subject:

4. Kammi and her mother (send, sends) emails nearly every day.

SENTENCE COMBINING:

5. The cake is in the oven.
   The cake is for Molly's birthday.
   The cake is chocolate.

   _____

   _____

DAY 99

CAPITALIZATION:

1. cindy asked, "is the dey mansion in new jersey?"

PUNCTUATION:

2. No these cookies dont require one half teaspoon of baking soda

PARTS OF SPEECH: PRONOUNS

Possessive pronouns show ownership. *My, mine, his, her, hers, our, ours, your, yours, its, their,* **and** *whose* **are possessive pronouns.**

Write an appropriate possessive pronoun:

3. Is that _____ bike?

ALPHABETIZING:

Write these words in alphabetical order:

4. queen   oval   rice   quake   rhyme   prance

   (a) _____   (d) _____
   (b) _____   (e) _____
   (c) _____   (f) _____

SENTENCE COMBINING:

5. His mother put drops in his ear.
   He has an ear infection.
   His name is Richard.

   _____

   _____

DAY 100

CAPITALIZATION:

1. the driver from norway turned south near opoe store in cherry valley.

PUNCTUATION:

Underline the names of ships, planes, and trains.
Example: <u>Spruce Goose</u> (airplane)

2. Lisa isnt the Monitor the name of a famous ship

DIRECT OBJECTS:

A direct object receives the action of a verb.
Tama threw a ball.
Tama, the subject, threw an object.
What is the object she threw? *ball*
Ball is called a direct object.

Underline the subject once and the verb twice. Circle the direct object:

3. Ginny diced red peppers.

PARTS OF SPEECH: PRONOUNS

Circle the correct answer:

4. (My friend and me, My friend and I, Me and my friend) like ice hockey.

SENTENCE COMBINING:

5. The children bought their dad a gift.
    The gift was for Father's Day.
    The gift was a book.

_____

_____

DAY 101

CAPITALIZATION:

1. james is a welder at fireside welding shop in loganville.

PUNCTUATION:

2. These riders are next   Tara Anne and Ricardo

PARTS OF SPEECH: ADVERBS
   Circle any adverbs that tell <u>where</u>:

3. Everyone rushed outside.

SUBJECT/VERB:
   Cross out any prepositional phrases. Underline the subject once and the verb twice:

4. Several dancers practiced for an hour.

SENTENCE COMBINING:

5. Eli scraped his knee.
   Peggy is cleaning the scrape.

_____

_____

DAY 102

CAPITALIZATION:
Capitalize the outline:

1. i. fish
       a. catfish
       b. trout
   ii. birds

PUNCTUATION:

2. My fathers friend wont be here until Sunday May 20

PARTS OF SPEECH: NOUNS
Write the possessive:

3. tools used by a cable installer - _____

FRIENDLY LETTERS: ENVELOPE
Write your return address on this envelope:

4. _____
   _____
   _____
   _____

   _____

SENTENCE COMBINING:

5. The water buffalo has wide, curved horns.
   The water buffalo has a very bad temper.

   _____

   _____

DAY 103

CAPITALIZATION:

1. "layla's parents went to dixie national forest," said parker.

PUNCTUATION:
Punctuate these titles:

2. A. (book) Corduroy

   B. (story) The Balloon

PARTS OF SPEECH: VERBS
Write the present and past tense:

3. A. **to listen:**
   1. Present: Today I _____ or he/she _____.
   2. Past: Yesterday Linn _____.

   B. **to do:**
   1. Present: Today I _____ or he/she _____.
   2. Past: Yesterday Linn _____.

PARTS OF SPEECH: VERBS
Cross out any prepositional phrases. Underline the subject once and the verb twice:

4. A bear and her cub sat by a quiet stream.

SENTENCE COMBINING:

5. An actress plays the part of Juliet.
   The actress is my sister.

   _____

   _____

DAY 104

CAPITALIZATION:

1. the dons club* visited sierra elementary school in december.

* name of club

PUNCTUATION:

2. Jack said   Theres an old fashioned trolley

PARTS OF SPEECH: NOUNS

Write a proper noun for each common noun:

3. A. town - _____

   B. state - _____

   C. sea - _____

   D. business - _____

PREFIXES/ROOTS/SUFFIXES:

A suffix is an ending. A suffix is added to a root.

   Example: coasted = coast + **ed**
                       (root)   (suffix)

4. The suffix of **merriment** is _____.

SENTENCE COMBINING:

5. The cat purred.
   The cat meowed.
   The cat darted across the street.

   _____

   _____

DAY 105

CAPITALIZATION:
 Capitalize these two lines from the poem, "A Bouquet for Mother":

1. she washed each flower face,

   and put them on the mantel

PUNCTUATION:
 Punctuate this friendly note:

2. Dad
       My new puppys bowl is out
    side Will you wash it and give
    him fresh water
                        Cal

PARTS OF SPEECH: NOUNS
 Circle any nouns:

3. A driver parked his car on a hill near the ocean.

PARTS OF SPEECH: ADJECTIVES
 **Adjectives can make comparisons.
 When comparing two ONE-SYLLABLE describing words, use <u>er</u>.
 When comparing three or more ONE-SYLLABLE describing words, use <u>est</u>.**
 Circle the correct adjective:

4. Lani is (shorter, shortest) than her sister.

SENTENCE COMBINING:

5. We went to the zoo.
   We saw a mother gorilla.
   We also saw her baby.

   _____

   _____

DAY 106

CAPITALIZATION:

1. yesterday, congressman romer spoke to us about the mexican war.

PUNCTUATION:

2. Who is your leader asked Carl

PARTS OF SPEECH: CONJUNCTIONS

3. The three coordinating conjunctions are _____, _____, and _____.

PARTS OF SPEECH: NOUNS

Nouns ending in ff usually add s to form the plural.
Example: muff - two muffs
Nouns ending in f sometimes change the f to v and add es.
Example: leaf - leaves
Nouns ending in f sometimes just add s.
Example: reef - reefs

Use a dictionary if you aren't sure.

Write the plural:

4. A. loaf - _____

B. plant - _____

C. gulf - _____

D. bay - _____

E. moose - _____

SENTENCE COMBINING:

5. The wagon is green.
The wagon is for hay.
The wagon is being pulled by two horses.

_____

_____

DAY 107

CAPITALIZATION:

1. a group who spoke only chinese toured hearst castle.

PUNCTUATION:

2. A. (poem)   McDingle McSquire

   B. (book)   Fred the Frog

   C. (story) The Flying Dwarf

PARTS OF SPEECH: NOUNS
Place a √ if the noun is abstract:

3. A. ___ wish
   B. ___ laughter
   C. ___ blister

PARTS OF SPEECH: ADJECTIVES

Adjectives often make comparisons.
Some two-syllable words add <u>er</u> (2) or <u>est</u> (3 or more) to compare.
   Examples: ugly   uglier (2)   ugliest (3+)
Some two-syllable words add <u>more</u> (2) or <u>most</u> (3 or more) to compare.
   Examples: recent   more recent (2)   most recent (3+)
Circle the correct adjective:

4. This is the (livelier, liveliest) puppy of the entire litter.

SENTENCE COMBINING:

5. Diana dropped a glass.
   The glass did not break.

   _____

   _____

DAY 108

CAPITALIZATION:

1. the belville fire department held a fair on labor day weekend.

PUNCTUATION:

2. In the field mice were eating corn

PARTS OF SPEECH: VERBS

   Underline the subject once and the verb twice.

3. She studied the menu and ordered soup.

PARTS OF SPEECH: ADVERBS

   Adverbs can make comparisons.
   If two items are being compared, use <u>er</u> for ONE-SYLLABLE adverbs.
   If three or more items are being compared, use <u>est</u> for ONE-SYLLABLE adverbs.

   Circle the correct adverb:

4. Manzo jumps (higher, highest) than I.

SENTENCE COMBINING:

5. This chair is broken.
   This chair is made of wood.
   This chair is yellow.

_____

_____

DAY 109

CAPITALIZATION:

1. did mother study about pocahontas in her history class?

PUNCTUATION:

Write the abbreviation:

2. A. February - _____   C. Avenue - _____

   B. Tuesday - _____   D. December - _____

PARTS OF SPEECH: ADJECTIVES

Circle any special adjectives called articles:

3. A banana and an orange lay on the table.

PARTS OF SPEECH: PRONOUNS

Possessive pronouns show ownership. *My, mine, his, her, hers, our, ours, your, yours, its, their,* and *whose* are possessive pronouns.

Write an appropriate possessive pronoun:

4. _____ neighbor is funny.

SENTENCE COMBINING:

5. Knights were sometimes given cash for their service.
   This cash was called scutage.

   _____

   _____

DAY 110

CAPITALIZATION:

1. the college student studied the shinto religion of japan.

PUNCTUATION:

2. Stephanies dad lives at 23 Cobb Lane Memphis Tennessee 38101

PARTS OF SPEECH: ADVERBS

Circle any adverbs that tell how or where:

3. She looked around nervously.

PARTS OF SPEECH: VERBS

Underline the subject once and the verb phrase twice:

4. Kit may have (brung, brought) his lunch.

SENTENCE COMBINING:

5. The first ice cream sundae was sold in Virginia.
   It was made with vanilla ice cream.
   It was covered with chocolate syrup.

_____

_____

DAY 111

CAPITALIZATION:
Capitalize the first word, the last word, and all important words in a title. Do not capitalize a, an, the, and, but, or nor unless it is the first or last word. Do not capitalize a preposition of four or less letters unless it is the first or last word. (Prepositions frequently found in titles include at, of, for, from, in, and to.)

1. last night, grandma read the cat in the hat to us.

PUNCTUATION:
Punctuate this outline:

2. I   Important holidays
    A   Memorial Day
    B   Armistice Day
  II Special Days
    A   Grandparent's Day
    B   Arbor Day

PARTS OF SPEECH: VERBS
Circle the correct helping verb:

3. (Can, May) I hold the door for you?

PARTS OF SPEECH: ADJECTIVES
Circle any adjectives telling which one(s):

4. Is this pencil darker than that pen?

SENTENCE COMBINING:

5. The chef made soup.
   The chef made a pie.
   The chef made potato salad.

_____

_____

DAY 112

CAPITALIZATION:

1. has senator angelo fann spoken to the kiwanis club lately?

PUNCTUATION:

Punctuate these titles:

2. A. (book)   What Spot?   C. (poem)   Pirate

   B. (story)   The Penguin   D. (magazine) Cooks and Cooking

PARTS OF SPEECH:

3. What part of speech is *Yeah!*? _____

SENTENCE TYPES:

Write the type of sentence (declarative, interrogative, imperative, or exclamatory):

4. A. I'm finished.   _____

   B. We're leaving!   _____

SENTENCE COMBINING:

5. The sugar bowl is an antique.
   Grandma bought it.
   She bought it at a tea room.

   _____

   _____

DAY 113

CAPITALIZATION:

1. last night brenda said, "i visited the golden gate bridge."

PUNCTUATION:

2. A business owners meeting will be held on Friday April 27

PARTS OF SPEECH: PRONOUNS
   Circle the correct pronoun:

3. Chan and Marco want (those, them) shoes.

PARTS OF SPEECH: NOUNS
   Write the possessive form:

4. a dog belonging to two girls - _____

SENTENCE COMBINING:

5. The plant dropped its leaves.
   New leaves then appeared.

   _____

   _____

DAY 114

CAPITALIZATION:

1. in washington, d. c., alex went to the jefferson memorial.

PUNCTUATION:

2. Eighty five tourists boarded a plane for Athens* Greece**

*name of a city
**name of a country

PREFIXES/ROOTS/SUFFIXES:

3. A. What is the root of **rehire** ? _____

   B. Is *re* a prefix or a suffix? _____

DIRECT OBJECTS:

A direct object receives the action of the verb.

                                       D.O.
            Example: He <u>baked</u> a **cake**.

Underline the subject once and the verb/verb phrase twice. Label the direct object - <u>D.O.</u>:

4. Jay opened the door.

SENTENCE COMBINING:

5. Mark is a dentist.
   Mark's office is in Vitter Square.

   _____

   _____

DAY 115

CAPITALIZATION:

1. a st. patrick's day party was held at kolb lodge in march.

PUNCTUATION:
   Place a comma between two adjectives that describe.
   Example: short, hollow bone

2. Yes I want a plump furry kitten

PARTS OF SPEECH:
   Circle the correct word:

3. Karen never takes (any, no) money with her.

SUBJECT/VERB:
   Remember: verb phrase = helping verb(s) + main verb
   Underline the subject once and the verb/verb phrase twice:

4. A storm is coming soon.

SENTENCE COMBINING:

5. The Native American told a legend.
   The legend was about the tribe's first warrior.

_____

_____

DAY 116

CAPITALIZATION:

1. a wedding was held at calvary methodist church in idaho.

PUNCTUATION:
Write the abbreviation:

2.   A. President - _____   C. centimeter - _____

     B. October - _____   D. Thursday - _____

PARTS OF SPEECH: VERBS
Write the contraction:

3.   A. they have - _____   D. she is - _____

     B. does not - _____   E. cannot - _____

     C. will not - _____   F. where is - _____

PARTS OF SPEECH: ADJECTIVES

Circle any adjectives:

4. A happy, laughing child sang funny songs.

SENTENCE COMBINING:

5. The rocking horse is painted blue.
   Jeremy is riding it.

_____

_____

DAY 117

CAPITALIZATION:

1. is pike's peak near colorado springs?

PUNCTUATION:

2. The brides gown had tiny shiny buttons

PARTS OF SPEECH: VERBS

Underline the subject once and the verb phrase twice:

3. Tim might have (ate, eaten) already.

PARTS OF SPEECH: NOUNS

Write the possessive noun:

4. A. a business belonging to one lady - _____

   B. a business belonging to several ladies - _____

SENTENCE COMBINING:

5. They went on a picnic in the forest.
   They picked up pine cones.

   _____

   _____

DAY 118

CAPITALIZATION:

1. my grandparents hiked in yellowstone national park recently.

PUNCTUATION:
Place a comma before a noun of direct address if it is placed at the end of a sentence.

        Example: Are you going, Jill?

2. Lets swim and play baseball Linda

PARTS OF SPEECH: PRONOUNS
  Circle the correct pronoun:

3. May Juan and _____ (I, me) take that?

SYNONYMS/ANTONYMS/HOMONYMS:

4.   A. Write a synonym for *wait*: _____

     B. Write an antonym for *wait*: _____

     C. Write a homonym for *wait*: _____

SENTENCE COMBINING:

5. The girl is water-skiing.
   This is her first time.

_____

_____

DAY 119

CAPITALIZATION:

1. in the 1960's, president kennedy toured a civil war battleground.

PUNCTUATION:

2. Write your friend's name with the last name first:

   _____

PARTS OF SPEECH: ADVERBS
   Circle any adverbs that tell <u>to what extent</u>:

3. She was very tired but quite happy.

PARTS OF SPEECH: VERBS
   Underline the subject once and the verb twice:

4. The barrels in the arena (falls, fall) over.

SENTENCE COMBINING:

5. Their father is a policeman.
   Their father works the night shift.

   _____

   _____

DAY 120

CAPITALIZATION:

1. mrs. lucash went to webster gallery located east of silverway freeway.

PUNCTUATION:

Punctuate this friendly letter:

2.   **(A)**   66 Lincoln Drive
                                    Whittier CA 90607
                                    May 20 20--

    (B)   Dear Mara

    (C)   Their thirty four friends will be arriving for their wedding next Saturday May 30

                                (D)   Sincerely
                                (E)   Dawn

FRIENDLY LETTER:

3. Label the parts of the friendly letter in #2: (A)_____, (B)_____, (C)_____, (D)_____, and (E)_____.

PARTS OF SPEECH: ADVERBS

Many adverbs tell *to what extent*. However, there are seven that are used frequently: *not, so, very, too, quite, rather,* and *somewhat*.

Write a sentence using an adverb that tells *to what extent*:

4. _____

SENTENCE COMBINING:

5. Carlo went to a store.
It was a grocery store.
Carlo bought popsicles.

_____

_____

DAY 121

CAPITALIZATION:

Remember:
Capitalize the first word, the last word, and all important words in a title. Do not capitalize <u>a</u>, <u>an</u>, <u>the</u>, <u>and</u>, <u>but</u>, or <u>nor</u> unless it is the first or last word. Do not capitalize a preposition of four or less letters unless it is the first or last word. (Prepositions frequently found in titles include <u>at</u>, <u>of</u>, <u>for</u>, <u>from</u>, <u>in</u>, and <u>to</u>.)

Capitalize these titles:

1. A. <u>the carrot seed</u>
   B. "a bicycle built for two"
   C. "dan and ann at the beach"

PUNCTUATION:

2. In fact theyre meeting you in forty five minutes

PARTS OF SPEECH: NOUNS

Circle any nouns:

3. Three cars sped around the raceway during the last lap.

PARTS OF SPEECH: VERBS

Underline the subject once and the verb twice:

4. A hot air balloon (rose, raised) slowly.

SENTENCE COMBINING:

5. Goats chew their cud.
   Camels chew their cud.
   Cows chew their cud.

_____

_____

DAY 122

CAPITALIZATION:

Capitalize the heading and greeting of this letter:

1.   77 lark lane
                                                             lancaster, ky 40446
                                                             january 13, 20--

   my favorite cousin,

PUNCTUATION:

2. I need to see these three students Teddy Aren and Billy

PARTS OF SPEECH: NOUNS

   A plural noun that shows possession and does not end in <u>s</u> adds an apostrophe (') plus <u>s</u>.
         Example: a horse belonging to two women - women's horse

   Write the possessive:

3. toys belonging to some children - _____

DIFFICULT WORDS:

   Circle the correct word:

4. A. (Too, To, Two) answers were given.
   B. I want to visit (their, there, they're) soon.
   C. (May, Can) we see that?
   D. Has the ground hog seen (it's, its) shadow?

SENTENCE COMBINING:

5. The family had a garage sale.
   The family sold an old bike.
   The bike sold for twenty dollars.

   _____

   _____

DAY 123

CAPITALIZATION:

1. either mrs. lopez or i will take easter baskets to hopewell hospital.

PUNCTUATION:

2. Our new address is 100 N Link Ave Wichita Kansas 67278

PARTS OF SPEECH: PRONOUNS
Circle the correct pronoun:

3. Did (her, she) do the project?

PARTS OF SPEECH: VERBS
**Tense means time.
Future tense means something will happen.** *Shall* **and** *will* **are used to express future tense. Use** *shall* **with** I.

Write P **for present tense,** PT **for past tense, and** FT **for future tense:**

4. A. ____ Ben **spends** most of his time hiking.
   B. ____ Tara **will stand** in line for us.
   C. ____ Our family **saw** ruins in the Southwest.

SENTENCE COMBINING:

5. Stella likes to draw animals.
   Stella's grandfather likes to draw animals.

   _____

   _____

DAY 124

CAPITALIZATION:

1. my cousin visited the pro football hall of fame in canton, ohio.

PUNCTUATION:
   Remember:
   Underline the names of ships, planes, and trains.

2. Jennys friends took the Eagle Express* on Monday Sept 4

*name of a train

PARTS OF SPEECH: VERBS
   Underline the subject once and the verb phrase twice:

3. We have (chose, chosen) a leader.

PARTS OF SPEECH: NOUNS
   Capitalize any proper nouns:

4. A. railroad   C. teacher   E. fido
   B. reading railroad D. berwick school   F. dog

SENTENCE COMBINING:

5. Miss Lee will attend the meeting.
   Miss Lee's assistant may attend instead of Miss Lee.

   _____

   _____

DAY 125

CAPITALIZATION:

1. a rocky seashore runs along acadia national park in maine.

PUNCTUATION:

2. Dr Tarn and his wife went to an A M A* meeting on July 21 2001

* abbreviation for American Medical Association

PARTS OF SPEECH: ADJECTIVES
Circle any adjectives that tell how many:

3. The six children waded in several puddles.

ALPHABETIZING:
Write these words in alphabetical order:

4. crash   dash   cash   clash

    (a) _____
    (b) _____
    (c) _____
    (d) _____

SENTENCE COMBINING:

5. Joyce is a gymnast.
    Her specialty is tumbling.

    _____

    _____

DAY 126

CAPITALIZATION:

1. marco said, "i've brought my chess set and citrustime* lemonade to the cookout."

*brand name

PUNCTUATION:

2. One woman spoke about calves lambs and colts at a ranchers meeting

SUBJECT/VERB:
Cross out any prepositional phrases. Underline the subject once and the verb/verb phrase twice:

3. He lay on the bed and yawned.

PARTS OF SPEECH: NOUNS
Write the possessive form:

4. a puppy belonging to three children - _____

SENTENCE COMBINING:

5. We went to a circus.
   We saw a lion jump through a ring.

   _____

   _____

DAY 127

CAPITALIZATION:

1. "my mother is a librarian at drew university," said tommy.

PUNCTUATION:

2. No youre not taking Spencers snake with you

PARTS OF SPEECH: PRONOUNS

Circle the correct pronoun:

3. Their dog jumps on (him, he) constantly.

PARTS OF SPEECH: ADJECTIVES

Adjectives often make comparisons.
Most one-syllable adverbs add _er_ when comparing two and _est_ when comparing three.   small   smaller (2)   smallest (3)
Some two-syllable words add _er_ (2) or _est_ (3 or more) to compare.
        Examples: pretty   prettier (2)   prettiest (3+)
Some two-syllable words add _more_ (2) or _most_ (3 or more) to compare.
        Examples: secure   more secure (2)   most secure (3+)

Circle the correct adjective:

4. A. This shade of pink is (lighter, lightest) than that one.

   B. My cousin is the (more timid, most timid) soccer player on the team.

SENTENCE COMBINING:

5. King Charles II gave land to William Penn.
   The land was in America.
   This happened in 1681.

   _____

   _____

DAY 128

CAPITALIZATION:

1. are horses allowed in grapevine recreational area?

PUNCTUATION:

Place a comma before and after an interrupter used within a sentence.
>Example: Your answer, of course, is right.

2. Sarahs first teacher I think was Miss Dow

PARTS OF SPEECH: VERBS

Cross out prepositional phrases. Underline the subject once and the verb twice.

3. The girl and her dog run before dinner.

PREFIXES/ROOTS/SUFFIXES:

4. What is the suffix of **teacher**? _____

SENTENCE COMBINING:

5. His grandfather works for a computer company.
   His grandmother works for a computer company.

   _____

   _____

DAY 129

CAPITALIZATION:

Capitalize these titles:

1. A. hill of fire

   B. "all summer in a day"

   C. pigs might fly

PUNCTUATION:

2. Is one third of the womans doll collection from London England

SUBJECT/VERB/CONJUNCTIONS:
Underline the subject once and the verb twice. Box any conjunctions.

3. The leader rose and waved.

PARTS OF SPEECH: VERBS
Circle any word that may serve as a helping (auxiliary) verb:

4. up   do   am   it   was   should   may   had   her   will

   might   for   were   did   from   so   would   are   were

SENTENCE COMBINING:

5. The play will be held in the auditorium.
   The play will begin at eight o'clock.

   _____

   _____

DAY 130

CAPITALIZATION:

1. the dads of tots club met to celebrate grandparent's day.

PUNCTUATION:

Plural nouns not ending in s, add an apostrophe (') + s to show ownership.
Example: one child
           two children   a children's playground

2. Yes several mices tails were curly

PARTS OF SPEECH: ADVERBS

**Adverbs can make comparisons.
Adverbs of two or more syllables usually use *more* (or *less*) when comparing 2 items and *most* (or *least*) when comparing 3 or more items.**

Circle the correct adverb:

3. He waved his second puppet (more excitedly, most excitedly) than his first.

PARTS OF SPEECH: VERBS

Underline the subject once and the verb that agrees with the subject twice:

4. That lady often (eats, eat) fresh vegetables.

SENTENCE COMBINING:

5. The sky was blue in the morning.
   It rained in the afternoon.

_____

_____

DAY 131

CAPITALIZATION:

1. a hindu temple was erected near new delhi*, india.

*name of city

PUNCTUATION:

2. Wow We did it Bobby

PARTS OF SPEECH: NOUNS
Write the plural:

3. A. calf - _____   D. bunch - _____

    B. bus - _____   E. plant - _____

    C. cry - _____   F. wax - _____

SUBJECT/VERB:

Remember: verb phrase = helping verb(s) + main verb

Cross out any prepositional phrases. Underline the subject once and the verb/verb phrase twice:

4. Some sheep were moved to a new field.

SENTENCE COMBINING:

5. Penguins waddled across the snow.
   Penguins also jumped into the water.

   _____

   _____

DAY 132

CAPITALIZATION:
Capitalize the outline:

1. i. land travel
   - a. train
   - b. bus
   ii. sea travel

PUNCTUATION:

2. A tall thin man greeted Mrs Begay and her son

PARTS OF SPEECH: ADVERBS
Circle any adverbs that tell <u>when</u> or <u>where</u>:

3. Janny often walks there with his dad.

FRIENDLY LETTERS: ENVELOPE
Write your return address on this envelope:

4. _____
   _____
   _____
   _____

SENTENCE COMBINING:

5. There are six lights in the kitchen.
   One of the lights is burned out.

   _____
   _____

DAY 133

CAPITALIZATION:

1. a boston church was erected near the winston hotel last may.

PUNCTUATION:
Punctuate these titles:

2. A. (book)   Our Family Tree
   B. (poem)   I'm Nobody
   C. (song)   Got Those Blues
   D. (newspaper)   Space News

PARTS OF SPEECH: VERBS
Underline the subject once and the verb phrase twice:

3. That diver must have (broke, broken) a record.

PARTS OF SPEECH: ADJECTIVE/ADVERB
Circle the correct word:

4. The clown juggles (easy, easily).

SENTENCE COMBINING:

5. The turkey was sliced.
   The turkey was placed in sandwiches.
   The turkey was barbecued.

_____

_____

DAY 134

CAPITALIZATION:

1. their race car was entered in the daytona 500 for the targo tire company.

PUNCTUATION:

Punctuate this friendly letter:

2.
                                        29999 Parkside Circle
                                        Braintree MA   02184
                                        Aug 9 20--

Dear Pippa
      I finally made a three layer cake It had coconut and chocolate frosting

                                        Your friend
                                        Bart

SYNONYMS/ANTONYMS/HOMONYMS:

3.   A. Write a synonym for *pale*: _____

     B. Write an antonym for *pale*: _____

     C. Write a homonym for *pale*: _____

PARTS OF SPEECH: VERBS

Circle the correct word:

4. Several dancers (don't, doesn't) have shoes.

SENTENCE COMBINING:

5. Cheese is a source of protein.
Cheese is a source of fat.
Cheese is a source of some minerals.

_____

_____

DAY 135

CAPITALIZATION:

Capitalize these lines from the poem, "Over in the Meadow," by Olive A. Wadsworth:

1. over in the meadow,
   in the sand in the sun,
   lived an old mother toadie
   and her little toadie one.

PUNCTUATION:

Punctuate these titles:

2. A. (poem)   Holiday

   B. (story)   Tale of a Tail

PARTS OF SPEECH: VERBS

Underline the subject once and the verb phrase twice:

3. A tornado was (seen, saw) earlier in the day.

PARTS OF SPEECH: NOUNS

Place a √ if the noun is concrete:

4. A. ___ love   C. ___ kite

   B. ___ friendship D. ___ truth

SENTENCE COMBINING:

5. Their car is gray.
   Their car is new.
   Their car has bucket seats.
   Their car has fancy tires.

_____

_____

DAY 136

CAPITALIZATION:

Do not capitalize the name of a disease.
Example: chicken pox

1.   she asked, "did your grandmother ever have measles?"

PUNCTUATION:

2.   On the actors face lines had been carefully drawn

PARTS OF SPEECH: VERBS
   Write the contraction:

3.   A.   we shall - _____   D.   have not - _____

   B.   here is - _____   E.   would not - _____

   C.   they are - _____   F.   she is - _____

PARTS OF SPEECH: ADJECTIVES/ADVERBS
   Use *well* to explain someone's health.

   Circle the correct answer:

4.   I don't feel _____ (good, well).

SENTENCE COMBINING:

5.   The child misbehaved.
   The child threw herself on the floor.
   The child also screamed.

   _____

   _____

DAY 137

CAPITALIZATION:

Capitalize this letter:

1.
                                            11 bow lane
                                            phoenix, az   85015
                                            december 1, 20--

   dear cousin bo,

        i saw doby ranch last summer when visiting flagstaff, arizona.

                                            sincerely yours,
                                            jamie

PUNCTUATION:

2. Youre the last person to try Mr Novack

PARTS OF SPEECH: ADVERBS
Circle any adverbs that tell how:

3. Carol swims well for a beginner.

FRIENDLY LETTER:

4. Look at #1. In which part of a friendly letter is the date? _____

SENTENCE COMBINING:

5. The clothes are still damp.
   The clothes have been in the dryer for thirty minutes.

   _____

   _____

DAY 138

CAPITALIZATION:

1. has attorney gill met with her client in the adams county jail?

PUNCTUATION:

Punctuate this friendly note:

2. Jack
    Its not too late for you to join us on Satur day for our riders club picnic
                  Mano

PREFIXES/ROOTS/SUFFIXES:

Write the prefix, root, and suffix of *unhappiness*:

3.   A.   prefix - _____

     B.   root - _____

     C.   suffix - _____

DIRECT OBJECTS:

Underline the subject once and the verb/verb phrase twice. Label the direct object - <u>D.O.</u>:

4. She stirred the cake batter.

SENTENCE COMBINING:

5. A chickadee often swings upside down on a branch.
It does this to find insects.

_____

_____

DAY 139

CAPITALIZATION:

1. was cortez a spaniard* who conquered mexico?

*a person from the country of Spain

PUNCTUATION:
   Write the correct abbreviation:

2. A. foot - _____   C. inches - _____   E. Road - _____

   B. pound - _____   D. Governor - _____   F. meter - _____

PARTS OF SPEECH:

3. What part of speech is *Whee!*? _____

PARTS OF SPEECH:
   Circle the correct word:

4. Kyle doesn't have _____ (any, no) marbles.

SENTENCE COMBINING:

5. The first cookbook printed in America appeared in 1796.
   It was published in Connecticut.

   _____

   _____

DAY 140

CAPITALIZATION:

1. the middle school students discussed the boston tea party.

PUNCTUATION:

Plural nouns not ending in s, add an apostrophe (') + s to show ownership.
　　　　　Example:　　one ox
　　　　　　　　　　　two oxen
　　　　　　　　　　　two oxen's stable

2. Has someone added two thirds cup of water to the childrens activity dough

PARTS OF SPEECH:　　ADJECTIVES

Circle any articles and adjectives that tell which one(s):

3. Place the flowers by that cart.

SUBJECT/VERB:

Underline the subject once and the verb/verb phrase twice:

4. Each dancer performed and then bowed.

SENTENCE COMBINING:

5. Tad's bike is blue.
　　Tad's bike was a birthday gift.
　　The bike is a racer.

_____

_____

DAY 141

CAPITALIZATION:

1. they bought mexican hot sauce at miracle market*.

* name of grocery store

PUNCTUATION:
Punctuate this outline:

2. I Famous airplanes
　　A <u>Spirit of St. Louis</u>
　　B <u>Spruce Goose</u>
　II Famous ships

PARTS OF SPEECH: ADJECTIVES
Circle any adjectives that tell how many:

3. Some palm trees were planted in seven large planters.

PARTS OF SPEECH: VERBS

In an imperative sentence (command), the subject is not always stated. The subject becomes you, understood. It is written like this: (You).

　　　　Example:　Hold this.
　　　　　　　　　(You) <u>Hold</u> this.

Underline the subject once and the verb twice:

4. Smile.

SENTENCE COMBINING:

5. The coin is old.
   The coin is gold.
   The coin is valuable.

_____

_____

DAY 142

CAPITALIZATION:

1. the jewish nation of israel held talks near the red sea.

PUNCTUATION:
If a noun of direct address is within a sentence, place a comma before and after the name.

        Example: Do you know, Tessa, if we may begin?

2. Have you Connie ever been to a fiddlers contest

PARTS OF SPEECH: VERBS
  Underline the subject once and the verb phrase twice:

3. The kitten must have (drank, drunk) the milk.

PARTS OF SPEECH: ADJECTIVES
  Circle any adjectives:

4. Seven hungry cows ate the green leafy grass.

SENTENCE COMBINING:

5. The child crossed the street.
   The child first looked both ways.

   _____

   _____

DAY 143

CAPITALIZATION:

1. is the u. s. naval supply center near colonial parkway?

PUNCTUATION:

2. Dads company is located at 42 Dee Rd Atlanta Georgia 30345

PARTS OF SPEECH: ADVERBS
  Circle the correct adverb:

3. She kicks a ball (harder, hardest) with her left foot.

SENTENCE TYPES:

  Write the sentence type:

4. A. Is it raining?   _____

   B. It is raining.   _____

   C. It's raining!   _____

SENTENCE COMBINING:

5. The television was turned on.
   The show was about history.
   Brian was watching it.

   _____

   _____

DAY 144

CAPITALIZATION:

1. a quilt entitled "fair grounds" is at the smithsonian institution.

PUNCTUATION:

2. Cindy exclaimed Youre the best

SENTENCES/FRAGMENTS:

A sentence contains a subject and a verb. It expresses a complete thought.
A fragment is missing a subject or verb. It doesn't express a complete thought.

Place a √ if the group of words is a fragment:

3. A. _____   Ice formed on the pond.

   B. _____   The actor in the middle of the scene.

   C. _____   Had her car serviced.

PARTS OF SPEECH: ADJECTIVES/ADVERBS
Circle the correct word:

4. He brushed his teeth _____ (good, well).

SENTENCE COMBINING:

5. A boy rushed through the crowd.
   He was excited.
   He shouted to his friend.

   _____

   _____

DAY 145

CAPITALIZATION:

1. his sister said, "their club toured the hancock house in maryland."

PUNCTUATION:

2. A light cool breeze blew through those campers site

PARTS OF SPEECH: ADJECTIVES
   Circle the correct adjective:

3. This woven fabric is (prettier, prettiest) than that soft satin.

PARTS OF SPEECH: VERBS
   Write the tense of the verb:

4. A. Mary **walks** to the market. _____

   B. We **will wait** for you. _____

   C. Cal **walked** his dog. _____

SENTENCE COMBINING:

5. Wrap the present in blue paper.
   Add a white bow.
   The present is for Tara.

   _____

   _____

DAY 146

CAPITALIZATION:

1. an atlanta policeman was taken to memorial hospital on tuesday.

PUNCTUATION:

2. Have you Tony ever heard of a plane called Sky King

PARTS OF SPEECH: NOUNS
   Circle any common noun:

3. A. book   C. Duke   E. canary
    B. tape   D. bird   F. Canada

DIFFICULT WORDS:
   Circle the correct word:

4. A. (You're, Your) the winner.
    B. The boys are going with (they're, their, there) leader.
    C. Do you know if (its, it's) Monday?
    D. The loggers have already left (their, there, they're).
    E. (Two, Too, To) much snow has fallen!

SENTENCE COMBINING:

5. The sunglasses are on the counter.
   The sunglasses belong to Jim.
   The counter is tiled.

   _____

   _____

DAY 147

CAPITALIZATION:

1. last summer captain doug bayn visited the astrodome in houston.

PUNCTUATION:

2. I love it   exclaimed Nicki

DIRECT OBJECTS:

Underline the subject once and the verb/verb phrase twice. Label any direct object - <u>D.O.</u>:

3. A horse ate an apple.

PARTS OF SPEECH: VERBS

Write the present, past, and past participle:

	present	past	past participle
4. A. to run -	_____	_____	(had) _____
B. to eat -	_____	_____	(had) _____
C. to see -	_____	_____	(had) _____

SENTENCE COMBINING:

5. Lori took a trip.
   Lori went to England.
   Lori went with her grandmother.

   _____

   _____

DAY 148

CAPITALIZATION:

1. the mayor and senator gert dined at a san francisco hotel.

PUNCTUATION:

2. Kari said The guest speaker for the hikers club has arrived

PARTS OF SPEECH: PRONOUNS
  Circle the correct pronoun:

3. A. The shopper and _____ (she, her) went into a store.

    B. This magazine is for _____ (we, us).

    C. This book was given to _____ (I, me).

PARTS OF SPEECH: NOUNS
  Write the plural:

4. A. wolf - _____   D. library - _____

    B. iris - _____   E. crash - _____

    C. stable - _____   F. volley - _____

SENTENCE COMBINING:

5. The dog is a St. Bernard.
    The dog is friendly.
    The dog often jumps over the fence.
    _____
    _____

DAY 149

CAPITALIZATION:

1. the movie, anna and the little ones, was playing at riverview theater.

PUNCTUATION:

2. Marys dad her uncle and her cousin went to Bangor Maine

SUBJECT/VERB:

Remember: verb phrase = helping verb(s) + main verb

Cross out any prepositional phrases. Underline the subject once and the verb/verb phrase twice:

3. Many of the flowers have already bloomed.

PARTS OF SPEECH: ADVERBS

Circle any adverbs that tell to what extent:

4. I saw a very tiny mouse scamper across a rather old bridge.

SENTENCE COMBINING:

5. The bicycle was in the driveway.
   The bicycle belongs to Heidi.
   The driveway is at the school.

_____

_____

DAY 150

CAPITALIZATION:

1. does the march of dimes association send out easter seals?

PUNCTUATION:

2. Write the last name and then the first name of a United States President:

   _____

PARTS OF SPEECH: VERBS

   Regular verbs form the past tense by adding the suffix, <u>ed</u>. Irregular verbs do not.

   Place a √ if the verb is regular:

3. A. _____ to toss   D. _____ to freeze

   B. _____ to throw   E. _____ to grab

   C. _____ to be   F. _____ to fill

PARTS OF SPEECH: ADVERBS/ADJECTIVES

   Circle the correct word:

4. That chef bakes very (good, well).

SENTENCE COMBINING:

5. The copy machine is broken.
   A paper is jammed in the machine.
   Ms. Sax is repairing it.

   _____

   _____

DAY 151

CAPITALIZATION:

1. is the tournament of roses parade held in pasadena each year?

PUNCTUATION:

2. I need the following items for my project   a glue wand a shirt and twenty six stars

PARTS OF SPEECH: NOUNS
Circle any nouns:

3. Mandy took pens, pencils, and a notebook with her.

ALPHABETIZING:
Write these words in alphabetical order:

4. supply   tub   sudden   truth

   (a) _____
   (b) _____
   (c) _____
   (d) _____

SENTENCE COMBINING:

5. A lemon is a citrus fruit.
   A lime is a citrus fruit.
   An orange is a citrus fruit.
   A grapefruit is a citrus fruit.
   A kumquat is a citrus fruit.

   _____

   _____

DAY 152

CAPITALIZATION:

1. jina went to china to study the buddhistic religion last autumn.

PUNCTUATION:

Punctuate this friendly letter:

2.
         (A) 957 S Iron Street
               Broomall PA 19008
               December 31 20--

  (B) Dear Ryan

  (C) Capt Lewis and I will arrive at 5 00 next Thursday January 5

          (D) Always
          (E) Mario

FRIENDLY LETTER:

3. The parts of the above friendly letter are: (A)_____, (B)_____, (C)_____, (D)_____, and (E)_____.

PARTS OF SPEECH: ADVERBS

Circle any adverbs that tell <u>how</u>:

4. He quietly gave the answer.

SENTENCE COMBINING:

5. The liver is an organ of the body.
   It helps the body in over five hundred ways.

_____

_____

DAY 153

CAPITALIZATION:

1. an arthritis* patient saw dr. lang in his office at smith medical building.

*a disease

PUNCTUATION:

In a split quotation, place quotation marks around each part spoken. Place a comma after the last word of the first part and after the person speaking.

Example: "I believe," said Jerry, "that you are wrong."

2. My father said Kala is a good cook

PARTS OF SPEECH: VERBS

Write the present, past, and past participle:

	present	past	past participle
3. A. to speak -	_____	_____	(had) _____
B. to bring -	_____	_____	(had) _____
C. to wear -	_____	_____	(had) _____

PARTS OF SPEECH: INTERJECTIONS

4. Give an example of an interjection: _____

SENTENCE COMBINING:

5. Dr. Jobe is a veterinarian.
   Dr. Jobe vaccinates our cows.

_____

_____

DAY 154

CAPITALIZATION:

1. are the sierra madre mountains west of the verde river?

PUNCTUATION:

2. The ladies food booth without a doubt will be popular

SENTENCES/FRAGMENTS:

A sentence contains a subject and a verb. It expresses a complete thought.
A fragment is missing a subject or a verb. It doesn't express a complete thought.

Place a √ if the group of words is a fragment:

3. A. _____ At the children's zoo petted the lamb.

   B. _____ Sit down.

   C. _____ Abbie and Mattie during their stay in Madison.

PARTS OF SPEECH: PREPOSITIONS

Cross out any prepositional phrases; label any object of the preposition - <u>O.P.</u>:

4. The mayor lives in the white house on that lane.

SENTENCE COMBINING:

5. Daren will take Mrs. Gerb to the doctor's office.
   Daren's sister may do it instead of Daren.

_____

_____

DAY 155

CAPITALIZATION:

1. paul wrote about april fool's day in his english class at carter elementary school.

PUNCTUATION:

2. Yes our childrens chorus sang Daisy during their show

PARTS OF SPEECH: NOUNS
   Write the possessive form:

3. several plates belonging to Rory - _____

SYNONYMS/ANTONYMS/HOMONYMS:

4. A. Write a synonym for *poor*: _____

   B. Write an antonym for *poor*: _____

   C. Write a homonym for *poor*: _____

SENTENCE COMBINING:

5. The lady screamed.
   The lady was in the grocery store.
   The lady said that her purse had been stolen.

   _____

   _____

DAY 156

CAPITALIZATION:

1. later, judge worth arrived at the u. s. capitol for a tour.

PUNCTUATION:

2. The three pronged fork I believe is in that drawer

SUBJECT/VERB:

Cross out prepositional phrases. Underline the subject once and the verb/verb phrase twice:

3. At a company picnic, her mom grilled hot dogs and served lemonade.

PARTS OF SPEECH: NOUNS

Capitalize proper nouns:

4. A. gloves   C. anderson house restaurant

    B. markin theater   D. movie theater

SENTENCE COMBINING:

5. A new restaurant opened.
   Doug's brother works there.
   Doug's brother is a waiter.

   _____

   _____

DAY 157

CAPITALIZATION:

1. did admiral jones meet with president ford at camp david?

PUNCTUATION:

2. Did you see the sleek new boats Cindy

PARTS OF SPEECH: VERBS

Regular verbs form the past tense by adding the suffix, <u>ed</u>. Irregular verbs do not.

Place a √ if the verb is regular:

3. A. ____ to come   D. ____ to go   G. ____ to surf

    B. ____ to call   E. ____ to trick   H. ____ to fly

    C. ____ to fall   F. ____ to rise   I. ____ to burst

SENTENCES/FRAGMENTS:

Write <u>S</u> for sentence and <u>F</u> for fragment:

Remember: A fragment usually is missing a subject or a verb.

4. A. ____ Running down the road.

    B. ____ The coughed for nearly two minutes.

    C. ____ A hospital nurse entered his room.

SENTENCE COMBINING:

5. The floors are wooden.
The floors are stained.
The floors need to be sanded.

_____

_____

DAY 158

CAPITALIZATION:
Capitalize this friendly letter:

1.
                                                15900 rockland road
                                                wilmington, de 19803
                                                may 12, 20--

    dear luis,
        our club will visit the dallas museum of art in texas. i hope to see a painting by c. mattson.

                                                best wishes,
                                                dena

PUNCTUATION:

2. Missy asked   Arent my shoes heels too high

PARTS OF SPEECH: VERBS
Cross out prepositional phrases. Underline the subject once and the verb twice.

3. The director and her crew filmed the movie at night.

PARTS OF SPEECH: ADVERBS
Circle any adverbs that tell <u>when</u> or <u>where</u>:

4. Eventually the girls went inside.

SENTENCE COMBINING:

5. The group hiked for three hours.
    The group hiked into a canyon.
    The group ate lunch there.

_____

_____

CAPITALIZATION:

Capitalize the outline:

1. i. flags
       a. country
       b. state and local
   ii. banners

PUNCTUATION:

Punctuate these titles:

2. A. (book)   If You Give a Pig a Pancake
   B. (story)   The Potato Soup
   C. (movie)   The Wizard of Oz

PARTS OF SPEECH: ADJECTIVES

Circle the correct adjective:

3. He is the (more active, most active) triplet.

SENTENCE TYPES:

Write the sentence type:

4. A. Stand up.   _____

   B. Will you remember?   _____

SENTENCE COMBINING:

5. Amanda talks loudly.
   Amanda's sister is very quiet.

   _____

   _____

DAY 159

DAY 160

CAPITALIZATION:

1. does any guide for the lincoln memorial speak dutch?

PUNCTUATION:

2. Old Ironsides is the nickname of a ship in Boston Massachusetts

PARTS OF SPEECH: NOUNS
Write **C** if the noun is concrete and **A** if the noun is abstract:

3. A. ___ buffalo   C. ___ honesty   E. ___ love
   B. ___ garbage   D. ___ canal   F. ___ wisdom

PARTS OF SPEECH: PRONOUNS
Circle the correct pronoun:

4. John punched (I, me) playfully.

SENTENCE COMBINING:

5. Sherry purchased popcorn.
   The popcorn was in a bag.
   The popcorn was unsalted.

_____

_____

DAY 161

CAPITALIZATION:

1. "free polio vaccines will be given at metro mall on wednesday," said mr. vargas.

PUNCTUATION:

2. During the party time was spent planning a trip to Paris France

FRIENDLY LETTERS: ENVELOPE
Write your return address on this envelope:

3.
_____
_____
_____
_____

_____

PARTS OF SPEECH: VERBS
Write the contraction:

4. A. must not - _____   D. cannot - _____

    B. you will - _____   E. who is - _____

    C. I would - _____   F. would not - _____

SENTENCE COMBINING:

5. Dark clouds rolled in.
    Some rain began to fall.
    The rain fell for an hour.

_____

_____

DAY 162

CAPITALIZATION:

Capitalize these lines of poetry:

1. in a shoe box stuffed in an old nylon stocking

   sleeps the baby mouse I found in the meadow

PUNCTUATION:

Use underlining or quotation marks:

2. A. (book)   Suzanne
   B. (ship)   Titanic
   C. (chapter)   Writing

PARTS OF SPEECH: VERBS

Underline the subject once; place two lines under the verb that agrees with the subject:

3. Her mother and dad (race, races).

PREFIXES/ROOTS/SUFFIXES:

Write the prefix, root and suffix of *redoing*:

4. A. prefix - _____
   B. root - _____
   C. suffix - _____

SENTENCE COMBINING:

5. The car is white.
   The car was speeding.
   The car has a dent in it.

   _____

   _____

DAY 163

CAPITALIZATION:

1. micah said, "in june, mom fished at lake mohawk in new jersey."

PUNCTUATION:
Remember:
In a split quotation, place quotation marks around each part spoken. Place a comma after the last word of the first part and after the person speaking.

Example: "I believe," said Jerry, "that you are correct."

2. Today said Maria isnt Tuesday

PARTS OF SPEECH: ADJECTIVES
Circle any adjectives:

3. A quick brown fox jumped over the lazy dog.

PARTS OF SPEECH: ADVERBS
Circle any adverbs:

4. Suddenly, the ball was hit hard.

SENTENCE COMBINING:

5. The air is filled with smoke.
   A brush fire is burning.

_____

_____

DAY 164

CAPITALIZATION:

1. hunters from asia crossed the bering strait around 18,000 b. c.

PUNCTUATION:

2. Mr and Mrs Jacobs sell the following   yogurt ice cream and milk

PARTS OF SPEECH: ADVERBS
   Circle the correct adverb form:

3. Their fax rings (more frequently, most frequently) in the morning than in the afternoon.

PARTS OF SPEECH: VERBS
   Write the present, past, and past participle:

	present	past	past participle
4. A. to smile -	_____	_____	(had) _____
B. to go -	_____	_____	(had) _____
C. to grow -	_____	_____	(had) _____

SENTENCE COMBINING:

5. Before lunch, they shopped.
   They shopped at a factory outlet.
   They bought sweaters.

   _____

   _____

DAY 165

CAPITALIZATION:
Capitalize these titles:

1. A. the tale of peter rabbit

   B. from seed to plant

   C. gumdrop has a birthday

PUNCTUATION:
Punctuate this friendly note:

2. Allie
       Youre invited to attend a writers break fast on Tuesday June 5
                         Nikko

PARTS OF SPEECH: PRONOUNS

An antecedent is the word to which a possessive pronoun refers in a sentence.
    Example: **Sally** likes **her** cousin.
                Antecedent   possessive pronoun

Circle the possessive pronoun; box its antecedent:

3. The boy held a stick in his hand.

PARTS OF SPEECH: PREPOSITIONS

Cross out any prepositional phrases. Underline the subject once and the verb/verb phrase twice:

4. Sal will go down the elevator with Jerry.

SENTENCE COMBINING:

5. A security guard searched the parking lot.
   A security guard was looking for a stolen wallet.
   The wallet was not found.

_____

_____

DAY 166

CAPITALIZATION:

1. for breakfast, she ate canadian bacon and crispy's* corn flakes.
*brand name

PUNCTUATION:

2. The answer I think isnt twenty three Dakota

PARTS OF SPEECH: CONJUNCTIONS/INTERJECTIONS
   Circle any conjunctions; box any interjections:

3. Terrific! He's won a blue and gold ribbon!

PARTS OF SPEECH: VERBS
   Write the 23 helping (auxiliary) verbs:

4. d_____   h_____   m_____   sh_____   sh_____   i_____   w_____   b_____
   d_____   h_____   m_____   c_____   w_____   a_____   w_____   b_____
   d_____   h_____   m_____   w_____   c_____   a_____   b_____

SENTENCE COMBINING:

5. A lady washed her car.
   No one helped her.
   Her car was new.

   _____

   _____

DAY 167

CAPITALIZATION:

1. mrs. dil teaches science at adams junior high school on west log street.

PUNCTUATION:

2. Ouch   Those cactis stickers are sharp

PARTS OF SPEECH: ADVERBS
   Circle any adverbs that tell how:

3. Those children put the puzzle together well.

PARTS OF SPEECH: PRONOUNS
   An antecedent is the word to which a possessive pronoun refers in a sentence.
   Example: I sometimes eat **my** lunch with my friends.
   Antecedent   possessive pronoun
   Circle the possessive pronoun; box its antecedent:

4. The neighbors left their car outside.

SENTENCE COMBINING:

5. Juan bought a hot dog.
   He put onions on it.
   He put mustard on it.
   He put pickles on it.

   _____

   _____

DAY 168

CAPITALIZATION:

1. is fingal's cave located on staffa island off western scotland*?

* name of country

PUNCTUATION:
   Punctuate this outline:

2. I   Mountains
      A   Rockies
      B   Appalachians
   II Rivers
      A   Colorado
      B   Rio Grande

PARTS OF SPEECH: NOUNS
   Write the possessive:

3. a pig belonging to more than one child - _____

PARTS OF SPEECH: ADJECTIVES
   Circle any adjectives:

4. Two young ladies scooped water from that sinking boat.

SENTENCE COMBINING:

5. Their grass is brown.
   It also has not rained recently.

   _____

   _____

DAY 169

CAPITALIZATION:

1. marsha asked, "did the governor visit buckingham palace last summer?"

PUNCTUATION:

   Punctuate this friendly letter:

2.   2 Doe Street
                                      Scottsdale Arizona 85254   **(A)**
                                      March 7 20--

   Dear Ed   **(B)**

       How are you doing   Well see you in a few months   **(C)**

                                      Your friend   **(D)**
                                      Danno   **(E)**

FRIENDLY LETTER:

3. The parts of the friendly letter in #2 are: (A)_____, (B)_____, (C)_____, (D)_____, and (E)_____.

SUBJECT/VERB:

   Cross out any prepositional phrases. Underline the subject once and the verb or verb phrase twice.

4. Two crocks and a wire basket are under the workbench.

SENTENCE COMBINING:

5. His lunch box is blue.
   His lunch box is shaped like a radio.
   The lunch box does not play music.

   _____

   _____

DAY 170

CAPITALIZATION:

1. in spanish class, we studied about the inca indians of peru.

PUNCTUATION:

2. Does Josh live at 34 Route 10 Succasunna NJ 07876

DIFFICULT WORDS:
   Circle the correct answer:

3. A. Is Jody going (to, two, too) her friend's house, (to, two, too)?

   B. What is (there, they're, their) favorite ice cream?

   C. Are you sure that (you're, your) ready?

   D. (May, Can) you wind this clock?

   E. I hope that (it's, its) not too late.

PARTS OF SPEECH: ADVERBS
   Circle any adverbs that tell <u>to what extent</u>:

4. I'm so hungry, but I do not want chips.

SENTENCE COMBINING:

5. Joel made an airplane.
   The airplane was made of paper.
   Joel flew the airplane across the room.

   _____

   _____

DAY 171

CAPITALIZATION:

1. their dad cooked eggs at bee rock campground last christmas eve.

PUNCTUATION:

Punctuate these titles:

2. A. (report)   Your Muscles

   B. (movie)   Benji

   C. (magazine)   Home Redo

PARTS OF SPEECH: VERBS

Circle the correct verb:

3. A. Hot air has (risen, raised) to the ceiling.

   B. Harry (set, sit) the food on the table.

   C. The cat is (laying, lying) on the bed.

   D. She (lay, laid) on a pool mat.

PARTS OF SPEECH: PRONOUNS

Circle any pronouns:

4. They left their money at home.

SENTENCE COMBINING:

5. A fitness center opened yesterday.
   Myra joined.
   It is very expensive to join.

_____

_____

DAY 172

CAPITALIZATION:

1. "does halo hair salon on beach boulevard sell wigs?" asked mrs. wong.

PUNCTUATION:

2. Youre the best   the man announced   in this division

PARTS OF SPEECH: VERBS

   Underline the subject once and the verb phrase twice:

3. A. The cowboy must have (went, gone) to a rodeo.

   B. Has the lawyer (brought, brung) her client?

   C. We should have (saw, seen) that.

PARTS OF SPEECH: ADVERBS
   Circle the correct form:

4. Of the three trains, the Rob Express travels (more slowly, most slowly).

SENTENCE COMBINING:

5. The bicyclist stopped to rest.
   The bicyclist rested on a park bench.

   _____

   _____

DAY 173

CAPITALIZATION:

1. is babe ruth's statue in the national baseball hall of fame and museum in cooperstown?

PUNCTUATION:

2. Ebony asked Wheres Doras note pad

FRIENDLY LETTERS: ENVELOPE

Write your return address and address the envelope to a friend.
(If you do not know a friend's address, make one up!)

3.
_____
_____
_____

_____
_____
_____

_____

PARTS OF SPEECH: CONJUNCTIONS
Circle any coordinating conjunctions:

4. The soda and pizza were ordered but not eaten.

SENTENCE COMBINING:

5. The belt buckle is engraved.
   The belt buckle is made of silver.
   The belt buckle belongs to a rancher.

_____

_____

DAY 174

CAPITALIZATION:

1. rick went to fort ticonderoga and learned about the american revolution.

PUNCTUATION:

2. Wow Ive jumped nearly four feet Mrs Moreno

DIRECT OBJECTS:

Underline the subject once and the verb/verb phrase twice. Label any direct objects - D.O.:

3. We ate doughnuts and drank juice.

PARTS OF SPEECH: VERBS

Write the contraction:

4. A. does not - _____   D. they are - _____

   B. we are - _____   E. did not - _____

   C. who is - _____   F. I am - _____

SENTENCE COMBINING:

5. Joe walked to the drugstore.
   Joe bought gumdrops.
   Joe also bought licorice and crackers.

   _____

   _____

DAY 175

CAPITALIZATION:

1. chad bought his guitar from sharp music supply during their winter sale.

PUNCTUATION:
Punctuate these titles:

2. A. (movie)   Fiddler on the Roof

    B. (book)   Tex

    C. (chapter) Insects

    D. (poem)   Evangeline

PARTS OF SPEECH: NOUNS
Write the plural:

3. A. memory - _____   D. reef - _____

    B. recess - _____   E. mouse - _____

    C. trace - _____   F. surrey - _____

SUBJECT/VERB:

Cross out any prepositional phrases. Underline the subject once and the verb or verb phrase twice:

4. May I open that gate for you?

SENTENCE COMBINING:

5. The pan is oblong.
   The pan is used for roasting.
   Mrs. Delany is cooking a turkey in the pan.

   _____

   _____

DAY 176

CAPITALIZATION:

1. shane said, "we attended the prescott music festival last july."

PUNCTUATION:

2. Kala I must buy these items for our trip sunblock a hat and a beach towel

SENTENCE TYPES:
  Write the sentence type:

3. A. Dad is home.   _____

   B. Dad is home!   _____

   C. Is Dad home?   _____

   D. Dad, come home.   _____

PARTS OF SPEECH: ADVERBS

   Some adverbs change form when comparing.
  Write the correct form:

4. Todd skied **well** on the first day. However, he skied _____ on the second day. Actually, on the third he, he skied _____.

SENTENCE COMBINING:

5. Millie's first answer was five.
   Millie's first answer was incorrect.
   Millie's second answer was right.

   _____

   _____

DAY 177

CAPITALIZATION:

1. during their hawaiian trip, a polynesian* luau was held at waikiki beach.

*referring to a place called Polynesia

PUNCTUATION:

2. Franny asked Is our girls volleyball team playing today

PARTS OF SPEECH: NOUNS

Place a √ if the noun is common:

3. A. ___ CLUB
   B. ___ COUNTRY CLUB
   C. ___ HILLCREST COUNTRY CLUB

SENTENCES/FRAGMENTS:

Write S for sentence and F for a fragment:

4. A. ___ Dressed in blue.   D. ___ The ran in a race.
   B. ___ We'd rather stay here.   E. ___ Come here.
   C. ___ The bus arrived early.   F. ___ Walking down the street.

SENTENCE COMBINING:

5. Salco Company is on Porter Avenue.
   Salco makes mirrors.
   These mirrors are for cars.

   _____

   _____

DAY 178

CAPITALIZATION:

Capitalize these titles:

1. A. prairie sisters

   B. "an apple for colliwobble"

   C. "barry has a fright"

PUNCTUATION:

Punctuate this envelope:

2. _____

   Lynn Batt
   12 Trow St
   Plano Texas   75074

                              Mr and Mrs Bob L Suite
                              Post Office Box 25601
                              Eagle Ridge NY   12057

   _____

PARTS OF SPEECH: NOUNS

Circle any nouns:

3. The back door of the house opens to a patio.

SYNONYMS/ANTONYMS/HOMONYMS:

4. Write an antonym for *partial*: _____

SENTENCE COMBINING:

5. He made cookies.
   The cookies have chunks of chocolate.
   The cookies also contain peanuts.

   _____

   _____

DAY 179

CAPITALIZATION:

1. his uncle gil owns an arabian horse in santa fe, new mexico.

PUNCTUATION:

2. The mens club will perform a short funny musical at 8 00

DIFFICULT WORDS:
Circle the correct word:

3. A. If (there, their, they're) ready, let's go.

   B. The cat licked (it's, its) paws.

   C. (You're, Your) guess was correct.

   D. I put (to, two, too) much soap in the laundry.

PARTS OF SPEECH: ADVERBS

Remember: Adverbs tell <u>how</u>, <u>when</u>, <u>where</u>, and <u>to what extent</u>.
Circle any adverbs:

4. Yesterday, a tired camel knelt down very clumsily.

SENTENCE COMBINING:

5. A book is on the floor.
   The book is about birds.
   Please pick it up.

   _____

   _____

DAY 180

CAPITALIZATION:

Capitalize this letter:

1.
   - **(A)** 10 brak lane
     chelsea, mi 48118
     december 12, 20--

   - **(B)** dear ricardo,
   - **(C)** we're looking forward to visiting shelter island, the zoo, and a mexican food restaurant.

   - **(D)** your pal,
   - **(E)** shelly

PUNCTUATION:

2. Taras mother needs ice lemons and sugar to make the drink

FRIENDLY LETTERS:

Label the parts of the friendly letter above:

3. A. _____   D. _____
   B. _____   E. _____
   C. _____

PARTS OF SPEECH: ADJECTIVES

Circle the correct form:

4. This race car driver is (more eager, most eager) than his partner.

SENTENCE COMBINING:

5. Taley's parents went to Ohio.
   Taley stayed with her aunt.

_____

_____

DAILY GRAMS: GUIDED REVIEW AIDING MASTERY SKILLS - GRADE 4
ANSWERS:

Sentence combining: Although only one or two possibilities are presented, other answers are acceptable. *Easy Writing* teaches how to write higher level sentences. For teaching grammar skills, *Easy Grammar* is recommended.

AMV/RA = ANSWERS MAY VARY/REPRESENTATIVE ANSWERS

DAY 1: 1. Have, Dr., Mrs., C., Winston   2. A. Ave. B. gal. C. Mr. D. ft. E. in. F. St.   3. (a) breath (b) cream (c) dart (d) dream (e) egg   4. <u>Janet sneezed</u>   5. AMV/RA: Her brother is making cookies for a bake sale.

DAY 2: 1. Has, Uncle, Mike, Miss, Diaz   2. Don't go.   3. A. isn't B. they're C. can't   4. AMV/RA: boy, Paul, policeman   5. AMV/RA: A library book is on the table. The book that is on the table is from the library.

DAY 3: 1. Their, Saturday, July   2. Wow! I won!   3. <u>band</u> <u>marches</u>   4. AMV/RA: spoon, bib   5. AMV/RA: Mark is sick today, and he had to stay home. Mark stayed home today because he is sick.

DAY 4: 1. My, San, Diego, California   2. Aren't we leaving soon?   3. AMV/RA: blue (cars), old (house)   4. <u>dog</u> <u>licks</u>   5. AMV/RA: The green and pink basket is broken. The broken basket is green and pink.

DAY 5: 1. The, Finland, Europe   2. Mira, Frank, and Chan were first.   3. b) admire   4. carefully   5. AMV/RA: The telephone rang, and Ted answered it. When the telephone rang, Ted answered it.

DAY 6: 1. Carissa, Austin, Texas, Tuesday   2. Tom, can you play?   3. today   4. I (subject)   5. AMV/RA: Tama fixed her bike's flat tire. When Tama's bike had a flat tire, she fixed it.

DAY 7: 1. Susan's, Hawaii, Christmas   2. Mary, have you been to Denver, Colorado?   3. down   4. interrogative   5. AMV/RA: The dish dropped and broke into many pieces. When the dish was dropped, it broke into many pieces.

DAY 8: 1. They, Ozark, Mountains, Missouri, August   2. He was born on Oct. 20, 1980.   3. A. and B. or C. but   4. White (clouds), fluffy (clouds), iron (bed)   5. AMV/RA: Joe's mom and dad are dentists. Both Joe's mom and dad are dentists.

DAY 9:
1. **Dear M**arco,
     Terry and **I** will visit **F**ish **L**ake next **T**hursday.
                                   Brian
2. Tara and I visited Anaheim, California.   3. A. interrogative B. declarative
4. <u>horse</u> <u>chews</u>   5. AMV/RA: The roses were blooming, but the daisies were not. Although the roses were blooming, the daisies were not.

DAY 10:   1. Is, Bighorn, Falls, Marsh, Peak   2. Maria, Frank, and Laylah left early.   3. Their (Their dad)   4. AMV/RA: at his funny remark*
5. AMV/RA: Jason mailed a letter for his dad. Jason mailed his dad's letter.

*__*Note:__ Students will eventually be asked to cross out prepositional phrases to simplify identification of subject and verb. You may want to explain this concept and provide a list of prepositions.

The prepositional approach to grammar is explained in ***EASY GRAMMAR: Grades 4 and 5*** by Wanda C. Phillips. An ordering address is provided on the back cover of this textbook.

DAY 11:
1. **Dear J**anny,
     We are going to **G**rand **I**sland in **J**une.
                    Your friend,
                    Tony
2. We took our pet to the clinic at 10:15 on Monday, August 3.   3. A. shouldn't B. aren't C. he'll D. I'm E. I've F. won't   4. aunt, puppy, home
5. AMV/RA: Two students washed the dusty chalkboard. Because the chalkboard was dusty, two students washed it.

DAY 12:   1. The, Dr., Begay, Blackstone, Virginia   2. Dear Mrs. Tate,
3. Cold (cold sandwiches), chocolate (chocolate cake)   4. a) clear
5. AMV/RA: Jane's ten-year-old brother is on the swim team. Jane's brother, who is ten years old, is on the swim team.

DAY 13:   1. We, Memorial, Day, May   2. My aunt's graduation party was Saturday, June 17, 2000.   3. A. to B. at C. in D. on E. for F. from G. by H. with I. up   4. A. √ B. √ C. _   5. AMV/RA: A carriage that was decorated with flowers was pulled by a horse. A carriage pulled by a horse was decorated with flowers.

DAY 14:   1. We, Old, Mill, Lane, Turkey, Creek   2. Molly, our bus won't leave until 7:00.   3. big (big balloons), blue (blue balloons)   4. A. √ B. _ C. √
5. AMV/RA: The Spanish brought figs, dates, and citrus fruits to America.

DAY 15: 1. The, Smith, East, Ball, Street, Reno, Nevada   2. Yikes! Timmy's snake is lost!   3. cat <u>sneezes</u>   4. at a diner   5. AMV/RA: When Ken skied for two hours, he fell three times.   Ken skied for two hours, and he fell three times.

DAY 16: 1. Was, Virginia, United, States, America
2. Dear Ben,
    I'll meet you soon.
        Your friend,
        Mickey
3. pig <u>oinks</u>   4. A. student's name   B. I   5. AMV/RA: In colonial days, carrot juice and salt were often added to butter.   Carrot juice and salt were often added to butter during colonial days.

DAY 17: 1. Senator, Tang, Santa, Ana, Freeway   2. Does Sally's uncle live at 4 Cedar Road, Cleveland, Ohio?   3. Your (Your pad)   4. interrogative   5. AMV/RA: David will repair the broken television after school.   The television is broken, but David will repair it after school.

DAY 18: 1. Matt's, Prime, Bank, Colt, Street   2. Miss Stoner, may I carry your box?   3. from your friend   4. a, the, an   5. AMV/RA: The children wore bathing suits, sandals, and hats.

DAY 19: 1. They, Yuma, Desert, Mexico, April   2. Bob's mother flew to St. Augustine, Florida.   3. Josh and I   4. tie <u>matches</u>   5. AMV/RA: A deer ate grass in a wide green meadow.

DAY 20: 1. Mr., Jay, Wells, College, September   2. Can't we spend twenty-five dollars on their gift?   3. <u>We</u> <u>clapped</u>   4. shirt, closet   5. AMV/RA: A Utah teacher spoke about Indian life.   A teacher from Utah spoke about Indian life.

DAY 21: 1. Does, Steve, Sax, Los, Angeles, Dodgers   2. Yes, Tammy's dog had puppies.   3. horse <u>lifted</u>   4. bold   5. AMV/RA: The toddlers were playing with yellow and red toy cars.   The toddlers were playing with toy cars that were yellow and red.

DAY 22: 1. He, Clifford, Takes, Trip, Pinto, Library   2. No, my uncle doesn't live in Orlando, Florida.   3. (a) smoke (b) strut (c) sung (d) track (e) vent   4. in the oven; object of the preposition = oven   5. AMV/RA: The eagle is perching on a dead tree limb.   The eagle is perching on a limb of a dead tree.

DAY 23: 1. Is, Penn, State, University, Nittany, Mountains

2.   I. Idaho
        A. Land
        B. People
3. may   4. fast, carefully   5. AMV/RA: A basket of bright yellow flowers is hanging on her patio.

DAY 24:   1. A, Fann, Company
2. Dear Vivian,
       How's the summer going for you?
                   A friend always,
                       Candy
3. early, late   4. A. exclamatory B. imperative   5. AMV/RA: The trees in autumn were dropping their leaves.   Because it was autumn, the leaves were dropping their leaves.

DAY 25:   1. On, Valentine's, Day, Aunt, Nina, Savoy, Candy, Store   2. We need two eggs, butter, and one-half cup of milk for the cookies.   3. its (its tail)
4. A. friend B. Elizabeth C. Iowa D. November E. valley F. Monday
5. AMV/RA: Lily likes to ski, sled, and ice skate. Lily not only enjoys skiing and sledding, but she also likes ice skating.

DAY 26:
1.   I. **D**esert animals
        A. **R**attlesnakes
        B. **T**urtles
2.   Our new address is 12 Link Drive, Biglerville, Pennsylvania   17307.   3. c) perfect   4. Those <u>trees</u> <u>sway</u> ~~in the wind~~.   5. AMV/RA: The Mayans had a system of writing and a 365-day calendar.   The Mayans had both a system of writing and a 365-day calendar.

DAY 27:
1. Dear Molly,
       Mrs. **B**ole will take us to **B**lackhawk **M**all on **T**hursday.
                   Your friend,
                       Chan
2. Yes, his name appears in the church's directory as Lima, Steve.   3. I
4. here, there   5. AMV/RA: The black and white butterfly is sitting on a tiny daisy.

DAY 28:   1. A. Monkey, Tales   B. The, Brave, Knight   2. We'll arrive at 9:00 on Saturday, July 14.   3. two (two classes), thirty (thirty children)   4. Hurray!
5. AMV/RA: The ice cream cone was introduced at the St. Louis World's Fair in 1904.

DAY 29: **1.** Carlos, Gumdrop, Seven, Lakes, State, Park   **2.** A. Dr. B. c. C. lb. D. Co. E. Dr. F. m   **3.** A. crashes B. printers C. stitches   **4.** A <u>man</u> <u>smiled</u> <s>at the baby</s>.   **5.** AMV/RA: When Aren rode his bike to Ted's house, they played chess. After Aren rode his bike to Ted's house, they played chess.

DAY 30:   **1.** Did, Texas, Falls, Vermont
2. Picnic items:
~ hot dogs
~ buns
~ chips
3. A. there B. your   **4.** A. <u>MV</u> B. <u>HV</u>   **5.** AMV/RA: Dad tripped over the toy that was lying on the floor.

DAY 31:   **1.** Last, India, Asia   **2.** During the storm, clouds rolled in.
3. A. √ B. _   **4.** c) arrival   **5.** AMV/RA: The dentist examined Fay's teeth, and she had no cavities.   When the dentist examined Fay's teeth, she had no cavities.

DAY 32:   **1.** The, Ohio, Senior, Olympics, Peck, Park   **2.** Did seventy-five people board the plane for Paris, France?   **3.** and, but   **4.** The scuba <u>diver</u> <u>arrived</u> <s>in a yellow car</s>.   **5.** AMV/RA: A soft gray kitten crawled onto Tom's lap.

DAY 33:   **1.** Does, Mayor, Dink, French   **2.** At night, time was set aside for camp games.   **3.** A. √ B. _   **4.** a, an   **5.** AMV/RA: The girls had fun washing the car.

DAY 34:
1.   **A** centipede was happy quite,
   Until a frog in fun,
2. Pam, add one-third cup of water to that soup.   **3.** A. √ B. √ C. _ D. _ E. √ F. _   **4.** few (squirrels), twenty (nuts)   **5.** AMV/RA: Mary Joseph Hale wrote "Mary Had a Little Lamb."   "Mary Had a Little Lamb" was written by the author, Mary Joseph Hale.

DAY 35:   **1.** Did, Japanese, Tippah, River
2. Dear Nick,
   We went fishing, boating, and hiking at a lake.
                                         Your aunt,
                                         Ama
3. <u>magazine</u> <u>has</u>   **4.** Darin and I   **5.** AMV/RA: The cheering fans watched a baseball game. The fans cheered as they watched a baseball game.

DAY 36:   **1.** A, Bee, Rock, Campground, Mercy, Hospital   **2.** Yes, I've made a three-layer cake.   **3.** by noon, object of the preposition = noon; on Friday, object of the preposition = Friday

4.
do	has	may	should	shall	is	was	being
does	have	might	could	will	am	were	been
did	had	must	would	can	are	be	

5. AMV/RA: An ant carried a piece of bread as it crawled across the sidewalk.

DAY 37: **1.** A, Pet, Palace, West, King, Street   **2.** They moved to 2 Peat Street, Plano, Texas.   **3.** A. imperative B. declarative   **4.** me
5. AMV/RA: A carnival to raise money for the fire department will be held soon.

DAY 38: **1.** A, Chinese, Birk, Union, Beach   **2.** A. but-ter B. re-play
3. A. Gulf of Mexico B. river C. lake D. Lake Erie E. Mississippi River F. street
4. striped (fish), blue (water), cool (water)   **5.** AMV/RA: When the boys raced, Dave won.   Dave won the boys' race.

DAY 39: **1.** Kyla, Mand, Middle, School, Atlantic, Ocean
2. 34 Lake Ave.
    Tucson, Arizona 85705
    January 23, 20--
3. A. don't B. I'll C. they're D. hasn't E. I've F. she'll   **4.** A. PR B. PA
5. AMV/RA: The small child who had an ear infection cried.   The small child cried because she had an ear infection.

DAY 40: **1.** One, England, Queen, Victoria   **2.** Janet said, "Take this with you."   **3.** Never (when), outside (where)   **4.** too   **5.** AMV/RA: Nani is reading a book with large, colorful pictures*.   Nani is reading a book that contains large, colorful pictures.

*Note: This is a good place to emphasize that a comma is used between two adjectives placed side by side unless one is a color or a number. (There are other exceptions, but this explanation will suffice at this point.)

DAY 41: **1.** Did, Pastor, Sells, St., James, Lutheran, Church   **2.** Millie asked, "When is the party?"   **3.** A. √ B. _ C. _ D. √ E. _ F. √   **4.** quietly
5. AMV/RA: The frisky puppy is chasing a ball.   The puppy who is frisky is chasing a ball.

DAY 42: **1.** A., T., Arkin, Chicago, December   **2.** No, Mike's parents didn't go to Naco, Mexico.   **3.** A. flashes B. classes C. envelopes D. taxes
E. bushes F. layers   **4.** loan   **5.** AMV/RA: The child sneezed, coughed, and took a tissue from the box.   The sneezing child also coughed and took a tissue from the box.

DAY 43: **1.** The, Eagle, Arts, Show, Wednesday, March   **2.** Let's meet at 2:00

on Thursday, February 19.   **3.** this (pencil), that (pen)   **4.** A. <u>do</u>, <u>does</u>, <u>did</u>   B. <u>have</u>, <u>has</u>, <u>had</u>   C. <u>may</u>, <u>might</u>, <u>must</u>   **5.** AMV/RA: The red car has a flat tire.

DAY 44:   **1.** A, Gleeful, Gardeners', Club, Ingle, Inn   **2.** Her name was listed as Bane, Penny S.
3. <u>should</u>   <u>shall</u>   <u>is</u>   <u>was</u>   <u>being</u>
       <u>could</u>   <u>will</u>   <u>am</u>   <u>were</u>   <u>been</u>
       <u>would</u>   <u>can</u> or <u>may</u>   <u>are</u>   <u>be</u>
4. few (few boys), one (one friend)   **5.** AMV/RA: Mary writes letters to her aunt and to her cousin. Mary writes letters both to her aunt and to her cousin.

DAY 45:
1. Dear **M**r. **F**lan,
        Your poem entitled "**T**he **B**ear and the **B**ee" is good.
                                Sincerely yours,
                                Meg **L**ewis
2. The clown said, "I'm making balloon animals."   **3.** AMV/RA: A. Heritage Park B. Syracuse C. Belgium   **4.** <u>Luke swims</u>   **5.** AMV/RA: Because my candy bar was left in the sun, it melted. My melted candy bar had been left in the sun.

DAY 46:   **1.** Micah, I, Topaz, Tile, Company, Zig, Avenue   **2.** They ate pizza, drank cola, and played ball.   **3.** <u>Holly works</u> ~~for a printing company~~.   **4.** Those (twins)   **5.** AMV/RA: Tracey couldn't find her sneakers because they were under her bed. Tracey couldn't find her sneakers that were under her bed.

DAY 47:   **1.** Did, Yosemite, National, Park   **2.** The R. J. Lincoln Co. opened last Thursday, Nov. 29.   **3.** (a) eating (b) fin (c) finish (d) grab (e) heat (f) inning   **4.** Tall (weeds), wilted (tree)   **5.** AMV/RA: My Uncle Phil teaches art at a junior high.

DAY 48:   **1.** Many, Americans, Veteran's, Day   **2.** Tina, did you add one-fourth cup of oil to these brownies?   **3.** view   **4.** tonight, tomorrow
5. AMV/RA: In 1850, settlers moved to Michigan, Wisconsin, and southeastern Iowa.

DAY 49:   **1.** Their, Glenrok, Art, Museum, Friday   **2.** Dad, where's Sen. Blatz going?   **3.** <u>clown sings</u>   **4.** A. puppies B. rays C. monkeys D. lobbies
5. AMV/RA: When Rob threw the ball, Sally caught it. Rob threw the ball, and Sally caught it.

DAY 50:   **1.** Is, Statue, Liberty, New, York, City, Liberty, Island   **2.** A. <u>Moby Dick</u> B. "Millie" C. "If" D. <u>Baby and Mom</u>   **3.** don't   **4.** Emma's map
5. AMV/RA: Chessa collects stickers, stamps, and shells. Chessa not only collects stickers, but she also collects stamps and shells.

DAY 51:
1. I. Schools
   A. Public schools
   B. Private schools
2. I need the following vegetables: carrots, potatoes, and onions.   3. inside
4. A. √ B. √ C. _   5. AMV/RA: Because Sally's lock was broken, she bought a new one. When Sally's lock broke, she bought a new one. Sally bought a new lock to replace her broken one.

DAY 52:   1. Little, Brad, Here, Comes, Snow
2.
                                        52 Elm Ln.
                                        Gettysburg, PA 17325
                                        May 8, 20--

    Dear Paco,
3. A. _ B. √ C. _ D. _ E. √ F. √   4. cousins visit   5. AMV/RA: We watched television and ate popcorn. While we watched television, we ate popcorn.*

*Note: Encourage students to think about higher level sentence structures. Be sure to share this pattern; students can learn by example.

DAY 53:   1. Last, Mrs., Kirk's, Elton, Circle
2. I. Arizona
   A. Climate
   B. Cities
3. may   4. conjunction = or; interjection = Whoa!   5. AMV/RA: The man, an artist, drew a picture of a clown.* The man drawing a clown picture is an artist.

*Note: The use of appositives is taught in *Easy Writing*.

DAY 54:
1.
                                        333 Strom Street
                                        Shippensburg, PA 17257
                                        April 22, 20--

    Dear Yancy,
2. No, Katie's pen won't work.   3. A (article), white (bunny), furry (bunny)
4. A. Their (teacher) B. its (paw)   5. AMV/RA: The delicious dessert was apple pie. The apple pie for dessert was delicious.

DAY 55:   1. Maria, Ted, I, Friday   2. A. "Mars" B. Summer of the Monkeys
3. in the middle, of the room, from China   4. A. PA B. PR   5. AMV/RA: The fractions test was difficult. The test about fractions was difficult.

DAY 56:   1. Miss, Dixon, Is, South, Mountain, Fair, September   2. Send the

box to 1 York Avenue, St. Paul, Minnesota 55101.   **3.** A. your (essay) B. two
4. A. boxes B. brushes C. sprays D. deer E. secretaries   **5.** AMV/RA:
Jana left the room because she was angry. Angry, Jana left the room.

DAY 57:   **1.** Did, Dad, East, Elm, Lane, Lubbock, Texas   **2.** Jana asked, "Are we leaving at 2:15 today?"   **3.** A. im B. not polite, rude   **4.** A. exclamatory B. interrogative   **5.** AMV/RA: The owl sat in a tree and hooted. Sitting in the tree, the owl hooted.*

*Note: This is a more difficult sentence combining. However, the concept of beginning with a participial phrase can be taught easily. Read about *Easy Writing* on the back cover of this text.

DAY 58:   **1.** Roy, This, Goody   **2.** Max exclaimed, "Yikes! We are lost!"
3. Several (children)   **4.** A. student's street address B. greeting (salutation)
5. AMV/RA: Because Gloria was shouting for her brother, she became hoarse. Shouting for her brother, Gloria became hoarse.

DAY 59:
1. I must not in play,
    Steal the birds away,
2. A. Mt. B. U.S. C. qt. D. m E. yd. F. Ln.
3. child's balloon   **4.** Joey, dad laugh   **5.** AMV/RA: The torn post card with the picture of a beach on the front is from our cousin.

DAY 60:   **1.** Have, Mr., Montoya, Dr., Jones, Top, Seed, Club   **2.** They've read twenty-seven pages of How to Eat Fried Worms.   **3.** Andrew, I fished
4. AMV/RA: A. may, will B. are, might be   **5.** AMV/RA: The bumpy dirt road has many loose stones. The dirt road with many loose stones is bumpy.

DAY 61:   **1.** They, Old, Mission, Lighthouse, Atlantic, Ocean   **2.** During the hurricane, wind was strong and gusty.   **3.** A. haven't B. you're C. he'll D. they've E. I'm   **4.** These (rods), that (net)   **5.** AMV/RA: The Spanish learned to make tamales from the Aztec Indians. The Aztecs taught the Spanish how to make tamales. Tamales were introduced to the Spanish by the Aztecs.

DAY 62:   **1.** Their, Alaskan, Blue, Moose, Lodge   **2.** Carrie exclaimed, "Look at that boat!"   **3.** A. boys B. crashes C. buzzes D. fields E. babies
4. They soaked ~~in a campground hot tub~~.   **5.** AMV/RA: While Mom made sandwiches, Dad made a salad for lunch. For lunch, Mom made the sandwiches, and Dad made a salad.

DAY 63:   **1.** The, Kline, Cactus, Cafe, Hoover, Mall   **2.** Mrs. Trueblood attended a popular songwriters' conference in a large Cali-fornia city.   **3.** I   **4.** blue (blue shirt), plaid (plaid skirt)   **5.** AMV/RA: Orange juice was served first, and milk was served later. Milk was served after orange juice.

DAY 64:   **1.** Ms., Tang, Florida, Bay, Dade, County   **2.** Place my name in the telephone book as Ross, T. M.   **3.** A. _ B. √ C. √ D. _ E. √ F. _   **4.** AMV/RA: A. reply, response B. first, initial   **5.** AMV/RA: Annie runs faster than Jack. Although Jack runs fast, Annie runs faster.

DAY 65:   **1.** Have, Sedge, Island, Ron
2. Dear Alicia,
    You're staying with us next summer.
              Love,
              Jenny
3. this (picture)   **4.** I chopped, fried   **5.** AMV/RA: Fifteen friends attended Randy's birthday party.

DAY 66:   **1.** Our, Franco, Food, Factory, Deer, Lane   **2.** Hasn't that chest's hinge been fixed?   **3.** do, does, did, has, have, had, may, might, must, should, could, would, shall, will, can, is, am, are, was, were, be, being, been   **4.** Their (Their uncle)   **5.** AMV/RA: The day was cold, sunny, and windy. Although the day was sunny, it was windy and cold.

DAY 67:   **1.** On, Independence, Day, Grandpa, Meese, Briar, Alley   **2.** They'll be leaving for Madrid, Spain.   **3.** *Answers will vary.* A. My friend has a snake. B. She has sent an email.   **4.** slowly, carefully   **5.** AMV/RA: Because Cameron has spilled lemonade, the floor is wet. Cameron has spilled lemonade, and the floor is wet.

DAY 68:   **1.** Their, The, King, I, Ramos, Theater   **2.** A. Tex B. "Cat and the Underworld" C. Friends and Family   **3.** She   **4.** Now, then   **5.** AMV/RA: Her brown curly hair needs to be combed.

DAY 69:   **1.** The, Aztec, Riding, Club, Bradford, County, Rodeo   **2.** A. Are you leaving? B. Please leave. C. I'm leaving. D. Yeah! We're leaving!   **3.** A. heading B. greeting (salutation) C. message (body) D. closing E. signature   **4.** proper   **5.** AMV/RA: We are going to the state fair next week. We will be attending next week's state fair.

DAY 70:   **1.** Was, George, Washington's, Mount, Vernon, Tina   **2.** Sally asked, "Where's Mike's new boat?"   **3.** few (squirrels), twenty (nuts)   **4.** anything   **5.** AMV/RA: Mrs. Lu is a pilot who owns an airplane. Mrs. Lu, a pilot, owns an airplane.*

*Note: Obviously, students can also write this sentence using a conjunction. However, this is another good place to discuss the concept of appositives. Students can learn by example.

DAY 71:
1.
                                        763 **E**ast **P**ark **A**venue
                                        Salem, **NC** 27108
                                        February 12, 20

      Dear **M**ario,
           We traveled through the **G**reat **S**alt **L**ake **D**esert to get to **S**ugar **C**anyon.
                                          Your pen pal,
                                            Pippa
2. May I join a girls' bowling team that plays at 6:00 on Thursdays? **3.** <u>have spent</u> **4.** A. Garnet Corporation B. Mummy Mountain C. newspaper D. Fido E. springer spaniel **5.** AMV/RA: A raccoon has a furry body and a long tail with black rings. A raccoon has a furry body and a long, black-ringed tail.

DAY 72: **1.** Does, Aunt, Bea, Jewish, Allied, Temple **2.** A. <u>The Star Tribune</u> B. "Storm Hits Area" **3.** A. holidays B. studies C. dishes D. melons **4.** <u>sit</u> **5.** AMV/RA: Crater Lake in Oregon is very deep. Crater Lake is a very deep one in Oregon.

DAY 73: **1.** He, Reems, Auto, Center, Monday **2.** Tami asked, "Have you read <u>The Staircase</u>?" **3.** I **4.** (a) main (b) mine (c) mist (d) nasty (e) netting (f) opal **5.** AMV/RA: I bought daisies from a flower shop that opened last week. That flower shop opened last week, and I bought some daisies.

DAY 74: **1.** Our, Austria, Richmond, International, Airport **2.** Good grief! We've added one-fourth cup too much vinegar! **3.** up, down **4.** <u>They have gone</u> **5.** AMV/RA: The pink ceramic vase was filled with straw. The vase filled with straw was a pink ceramic one.

DAY 75: **1.** We, Clear, Springs, Memorial, Day **2.** Kim said, "My brother is twenty-one years old." **3.** A. _ B. √ C. √ D. √ E. _ **4.** <u>boss must have given</u> **5.** AMV/RA: Joanie and her sister went ice skating on Bardton Pond. Joanie and her sister went to Bardton Pond to ice skate.

DAY 76: **1.** A, Christian, Bethlehem **2.** Candy, let's eat breakfast, clean our rooms, and ride our bikes. **3.** <u>aunt uses</u> **4.** A. Your (sunglasses) B. It's C. too **5.** AMV/RA: Danno's lunch consisting of a sandwich and cookies is in the refrigerator. Danno's lunch, a sandwich and cookies, is in the refrigerator.

DAY 77:
1. I. Lakes
       A. Fresh water
       B. Salt water
2. "You're our leader," said Artie.   3. A. exclamatory B. imperative C. declarative   4. bus's tires   5. AMV/RA: This new blue watch was given to Barbara as a graduation gift. For graduation, Barbara was given a new blue watch.

DAY 78:   1. Many, Burnsville, Children's, Festival   2. "What is a two-humped camel called?" asked Sharon.   3. and, but   4. Adanna, macaroni, cheese, lunch   5. AMV/RA: Mom and Dad caught five fish at a lake. When Mom and Dad went fishing at a lake, they caught five fish.

DAY 79:   1. On, Labor, Day, Rabbi, Good, Mono, Hot, Springs
2. Drinks for picnic:
       ~ lemonade
       ~ water
       ~ soda
3. a, the   4. <u>bride, attendants are</u>   5. AMV/RA: When the bike race began, I fell off my bike and skinned my knee.

DAY 80:   1. Did, Uncle, Bill, Hotel, Herald, Los, Angeles, Convention, Center
2. Her uncle's friend wants to live at 12 Main Street, Meredith, NH 03253.
3. on the roof, O. P. = roof; of our car, O. P. = car   4. lovingly   5. AMV/RA: The first Russian settlement in America was started in 1809 at Bodega Bay. America's first Russian settlement was started at Bodega Bay in 1809.

DAY 81:   1. The, I, Twirly   2. A. "Arise and Shine" B. <u>Roll of Thunder, Hear My Cry</u> C. "On a Rainy Day"   3. those (kittens)   4. Can   5. AMV/RA: His blue tennis shoes are lying in the corner of the room.

DAY 82:   1. A, German, Fort, Collins, Korean, War
2. I. Cats
       A. Persian
           1. History
           2. Habits
       B. Siamese
3. The <u>bus</u> ~~with flashing lights~~ <u>stopped</u>.   4. Wow!   5. AMV/RA: Tom's aunt who lives in Detroit is a social studies teacher. Tom's aunt, a social studies teacher, lives in Detroit.*

*Note: Easy Writing teaches how to write appositives. See the back of this text for more information.

DAY 83: 1. Did, Officer, R., B., Hood, Garden, State, Parkway 2. A. Fri. B. dept. C. Jan. D. c. 3. A. <u>PT</u> B. <u>P</u> C. <u>FT</u> 4. Cold (sandwiches), chocolate (cake) 5. AMV/RA: The palomino horse is named Colonel. The horse, a palomino, is named Colonel.

DAY 84:
1. **W**hen all the world is fast asleep,
   Along the midnight skies,
2. Dear Alonza,
       We found it fun to go to Rome, Italy.
   In the country, people sang many beautiful songs and entertained us.
             Ellen
3. <u>has run</u> 4. loudly 5. AMV/RA: The green wagon has black tires and a new handle. The wagon with green paint has a new handle and black tires.

DAY 85: 1. We, South, America, April, Ruth 2. By the way, she cuts both of my parents' hair. 3. These (shoes), that (dress) 4. <u>boys</u> <u>washed</u>, <u>dried</u> 5. AMV/RA: Because it rained all day, the children had to stay inside. The children had to stay inside when it rained all day.

DAY 86: 1. When, Liberty, Bell, Independence, Hall 2. "Don't go, (!)" pleaded Peter. 3. An <u>elk</u> <u>stopped</u> ~~by the road~~. 4. ful 5. AMV/RA: One monkey was sitting on a tree limb while another monkey was swinging on a rope. One monkey was sitting on a tree limb, and another monkey was swinging on a rope.

DAY 87: 1. A. A, Busy, Year B. Riding, Train C. Have, You, Seen, Bugs 2. "May I help you?" asked the clerk. 3. A. imperative B. interrogative 4. A. _ B. √ C. √ D. _ 5. AMV/RA: An invitation to Gail and Gabe's wedding arrived in the mail. Because Gail and Gabe will marry, an invitation to their wedding arrived in the mail.

DAY 88: 1. May, I, New, Zealand, Miss, Thon 2. Yes, Tommy's dad will arrive on Monday, July 30. 3. two babies' ball 4. later 5. AMV/RA: The first orange groves were planted at San Gabriel Mission in California around 1800. The first orange groves were planted at California's San Gabriel Mission around 1800.

DAY 89: 1. Captain, Sees, My, World, War 2. Did Cameo, Dan, and Erica watch a movie called <u>Sabrina</u>? 3. campers' tent 4. taller 5. AMV/RA: Jemima collects antique pillow cases with lace trim. Jemima's antique pillow cases in her collection have lace trim.

DAY 90: 1. Christina, Italian, Peace, Corps 2. student's last name,

student's first name   3. A. couldn't B. it's C. I'm D. can't E. won't F. what's
4. A. so B. too C. very D. quite E. rather F. not   5. AMV/RA: The woman opened the blueprint, laid it on the table, and studied it. After the woman opened the blueprint, she laid it on the table and studied it.

DAY 91:   1. The, Shoshone, Indian, Sacagawea   2. A. <u>Hairdos</u> B. "If" C. <u>National Report</u>   3. They're   4. My <u>grandpa is</u> ~~in that race~~.
5. AMV/RA: Cody made a noodle necklace in nursery school. Cody's noodle necklace was made in nursery school.

DAY 92:   1. Melissa, I, Africa, November
2.
                                31 Core Dr.
                                Birmingham, Alabama 35223
                                Sept. 27, 20--

Dear Ted,
        I'll be home for Thanksgiving.   Will there be thirty-two guests again?
                                Sincerely,
                                Bart
3. A. heading B. greeting C. body D. closing E. signature   4. prefix = dis root = like   5. AMV/RA: A daddy longlegs or harvestman is related to spiders. A daddy longlegs which is also called a harvestman is related to spiders.

DAY 93:   1. For, Thanksgiving, Mississippi   2. By the way, those golfers' tee time is 6:00.   3. A. faces B. stories C. flashes D. Sundays E. geese
4. me   5. AMV/RA: The check on the table is for your lunch. The check for your lunch is on the table.

DAY 94:   1. Every, Christmas, Eve, Rios, Bell, Mountain, Ski, Area   2. The Maj. R. Dobbs spoke about life in 1215 B.C.   3. A. AMV/RA: purchase B. AMV/RA: sell C. by, bye   4. anybody   5. AMV/RA: Because the glue stick was on the floor, Dakota picked it up. Dakota picked up the glue stick from the floor.

DAY 95:   1. Did, Mayor, Link, French, Pacific, Ocean
2. Sincerely yours,
    Mario C. Rubio
3. A. interrogative B. exclamatory   4. <u>family</u> had driven   5. AMV/RA: Milly and Cal are riding horses along a bridle path in a park.

DAY 96:   1. Has, William, Perry, Chicago, Bears   2. "That's two-ply bathroom tissue," said Miss Goya.   3. on Thursday and Friday; O.P. = Thursday, Friday
4. straighter   5. AMV/RA: Micah went to a bookstore and then to a hardware store. Before going to a hardware store, Micah went to a bookstore.

DAY 97:
1.   66421 Chapel Hills Drive
                                Colorado Springs, CO 80920
                                July 3, 20--
Dear Aunt Jenny,
     Let's go to Picadilly Square in London when we are in England.
                                Your niece,
                                Tanesha
2. After the snow, men plowed the roads.   3. A. it's B. you're C. too
4. One (One artist), many (many paintings)   5. AMV/RA: Sheri filled the empty stapler. When the stapler was empty, Sheri filled it.

DAY 98: 1. In, Senator, Cane, Chile, South, America   2. Susan, your dog is cute, friendly, and frisky.   3. riders' path   4. <u>Kammi, mother send</u>
5. AMV/RA: The chocolate cake for Molly's birthday is in the oven. Molly's chocolate birthday cake is in the oven.

DAY 99: 1. Cindy, Is, Dey, Mansion, New, Jersey   2. No, these cookies don't require one-half teaspoon of baking soda.   3. AMV/RA: your, her
4. (a) oval (b) prance (c) quake (d) queen (e) rhyme (f) rice
5. AMV/RA: Richard's mother put drops in his infected ear. Because Richard has an ear infection, his mother put drops in his ear.

DAY 100: 1. The, Norway, Opoe, Store, Cherry, Valley   2. Lisa, isn't the <u>Monitor</u> the name of a famous ship?   3. <u>Ginny diced</u>; D.O. = peppers   4. My friend and I   5. AMV/RA: The children bought their dad a book for Father's Day.

DAY 101: 1. James, Fireside, Welding, Shop, Loganville   2. These riders are next: Tara, Anne, and Ricardo.   3. outside   4. Several <u>dancers practiced</u> <s>for an hour</s>.   5. AMV/RA: Peggy is cleaning Eli's scraped knee. Because Eli scraped his knee, Peggy is cleaning it.

DAY 102:
1. I. Fish
      A. Catfish
      B. Trout
   II. Birds
2. My father's friend won't be here until Sunday, May 20.   3. a cable installer's tools   4. Students name/student's street address/student's town (city), state zip code   5. AMV/RA: The water buffalo has wide, curved horns and a very bad temper.

DAY 103: 1. Layla's, Dixie, National, Forest, Parker   2. A. <u>Corduroy</u>

B. "The Balloon"   3. A. 1. listen, listens   2. listened   B. 1. do, does   2. did
4. A <u>bear</u> and her <u>cub</u> <u>sat</u> <s>by a quiet stream</s>.   5. AMV/RA: An actress who plays the part of Juliet is my sister.   My sister, an actress, plays the part of Juliet.

DAY 104:   1. The, Dons, Club, Sierra, Elementary, School   2. Jack said, "There's an old-fashioned trolley."   3. A. AMV/RA: Auburn   B. AMV/RA: Louisiana   C. AMV/RA: Caspian Sea   D. AMV/RA: Fromala Day Spa   4. ment
5. AMV/RA: The cat purred, meowed, and darted across the street.   After purring, the cat meowed and darted across the street.

DAY 105:
1. She washed each flower face,
   And put them on the mantel
2. Dad,
       My new puppy's bowl is out-
       side. Will you wash it and give
       him fresh water?
                   Cal
3. driver, car, hill, ocean   4. shorter   5. AMV/RA: We saw a mother gorilla and her baby at the zoo.   When we went to the zoo, we saw a mother gorilla and her baby.

DAY 106:   1. Yesterday, Congressman, Romer, Mexican, War   2. "Who is your leader?" asked Carl.   3. and, but, or   4. A. loaves   B. plants   C. gulfs   D. bays   E. moose   5. AMV/RA: The green hay wagon is being pulled by two horses.   A hay wagon that is green is being pulled by two horses.

DAY 107:   1. A, Chinese, Hearst, Castle   2. A. "McDingle McSquire"   B. <u>Fred the Frog</u>   C. "The Flying Dwarf"   3. A. √   B. √   C. _   4. liveliest
5. AMV/RA: Diana dropped a glass, but it did not break.   The glass that Diana dropped did not break.

DAY 108:   1. The, Belville, Fire, Department, Labor, Day   2. In the field, mice were eating corn.   3. She <u>studied</u>, <u>ordered</u>   4. higher   5. AMV/RA: The yellow wooden chair is broken.   The yellow chair made of wood is broken.

DAY 109:   1. Did, Mother, Pocahontas   2. A. Feb.   B. Tues.   C. Ave.   D. Dec.   3. A, an, the   4. AMV/RA: Our, Your   5. AMV/RA: Knights were sometimes given cash or scutage for their service.   Knights were given cash called scutage for their service.

DAY 110:   1. The, Shinto, Japan   2. Stephanie's dad lives at 23 Cobb Lane, Memphis, Tennessee 38101.   3. around, nervously   4. <u>Kit may have brought</u>

5. AMV/RA: The first ice cream sundae, vanilla ice cream covered with chocolate syrup, was sold in Virginia. The first sundae(,) which was made of vanilla ice cream covered with chocolate syrup(,) was sold in Virginia*.

*Note: If the added information (relative clause) is important to the sentence, commas are not needed. This is a higher level concept and added only for teacher insight.

DAY 111:   **1.** Last, Grandma, The, Cat, Hat
2.   I.   Important holidays
         A.   Memorial Day
         B.   Armistice Day
   II.   Special Days
         A.   Grandparent's Day
         B.   Arbor Day
3. May   **4.** this (pencil), that (pen)   **5.** AMV/RA: The chef made soup, a pie, and potato salad.

DAY 112:   **1.** Has, Senator, Angelo, Fann, Kiwanis, Club   **2.** A. <u>What Spot?</u>
B. "The Penguin"   C. "Pirate"   D. <u>Cooks and Cooking</u>   **3.** interjection
4. A. declarative   B. exclamatory   **5.** AMV/RA: Grandma bought an antique sugar bowl at a tea room.

DAY 113:   **1.** Last, Brenda, I, Golden, Gate, Bridge   **2.** A business owners' meeting will be held on Friday, April 27.   **3.** those   **4.** two girls' dog
5. AMV/RA: After the plant dropped its leaves, new ones appeared. New leaves appeared after the old ones had dropped from the plant.

DAY 114:   **1.** In, Washington, D., C., Alex, Jefferson, Memorial   **2.** Eighty-five tourists boarded a plane for Athens, Greece.   **3.** A. hire   B. prefix   **4.** <u>Jay opened</u>; D.O. = door   **5.** AMV/RA: Mark's dental office is in Vitter Square. Mark is a dentist whose office is in Vitter Square.

DAY 115:   **1.** A, St., Patrick's, Day, Kolb, Lodge, March   **2.** Yes, I want a plump, furry kitten.   **3.** any   **4.** <u>storm</u> <u>is coming</u>   **5.** AMV/RA: The Native American told a legend about the tribe's first warrior. The legend told by the Native American concerned the tribe's first warrior.

DAY 116:   **1.** A, Calvary, Methodist, Church, Idaho   **2.** A. Pres. B. Oct.
C. cm D. Thurs.   **3.** A. they've B. doesn't C. won't D. she's E. can't F. where's   **4.** A (child), happy (child), laughing (child), funny (songs)
5. AMV/RA: Jeremy is riding on a blue rocking horse. The rocking horse on which Jeremy is riding is painted blue.

DAY 117: 1. Is, Pike's, Peak, Colorado, Springs   2. The bride's gown had tiny, shiny buttons.   3. Tim <u>might have eaten</u>   4. A. lady's business B. ladies' business   5. AMV/RA: During their picnic in the forest, they picked up pine cones.   When they picnicked* in the forest, they picked up pine cones.

*Note: <u>K</u> is added to <u>picnic</u> because the suffix begins with a vowel.

DAY 118: 1. My, Yellowstone, National, Park   2. Let's swim and play baseball, Linda   3. I   4. A. AMV/RA: pause B. AMV/RA: proceed C. weight   5. AMV/RA: The girl is water-skiing for the first time. This is the girl's first attempt at water-skiing.

DAY 119: 1. In, President, Kennedy, Civil, War   2. friend's last name, friend's first name   3. very (to what extent tired), quite (to what extent happy)   4. <u>barrels</u> <u>fall</u>   5. AMV/RA: Their father, who is a policeman, works the night shift.

DAY 120: 1. Mrs, Lucash, Webster, Gallery, Silverway, Freeway
2.
                                66 Lincoln Drive
                                Whittier, CA   90607
                                May 20, 20--
Dear Mara,
    Their thirty-four friends will be arriving for their wedding next Saturday, May 30.
                                Sincerely,
                                Dawn
3. A. heading B. greeting (salutation) C. body D. closing E. signature
4. AMV/RA: I am so sad about my lost cat.   5. AMV/RA: When Carlo went to a grocery store, he bought popsicles. Carlo bought popsicles at a grocery store.

DAY 121: 1. A. The, Carrot, Seed B. A, Bicycle, Built, Two C. Dan, Ann, Beach   2. In fact, they're meeting you in forty-five minutes. (!)   3. cars, raceway, lap   4. <u>balloon</u> <u>rose</u>   5. AMV/RA: Goats, cows, and camels chew their cud.

DAY 122:
1.
                                77 Lark Lane
                                Lancaster, KY   40446
                                January 13, 20--
    My favorite cousin,
2. I need to see these three students: Teddy, Aren, and Billy.   3. children's toys
4. A. Two B. there C. May D. its (shadow)   5. AMV/RA: The family sold an old bike for twenty dollars at a garage sale. The family had a garage sale and sold an old bike for twenty dollars.

DAY 123: 1. Either, Mrs., Lopez, I, Easter, Hopewell, Hospital 2. Our new address is 100 N. Link Ave., Wichita, Kansas 67278. 3. she 4. A. <u>P</u> B. <u>FT</u> C. <u>PT</u> 5. AMV/RA: Both Stella and her grandfather like to draw animals.

DAY 124: 1. My, Pro, Football, Hall, Fame, Canton, Ohio 2. Jenny's friends took the <u>Eagle Express</u> on Monday, Sept. 4. 3. <u>We have chosen</u> 4. A. railroad B. Reading Railroad C. teacher D. Berwick School E. Fido F. dog 5. AMV/RA: Either Miss Lee or her assistant will attend the meeting. Miss Lee or her assistant will attend the meeting.

DAY 125: 1. A, Acadia, National, Park, Maine 2. Dr. Tarn and his wife went to an A.M.A. meeting on July 21, 2001. 3. six (children), several (puddles) 4. (a) cash (b) clash (c) crash (d) dash 5. AMV/RA: Joyce is a gymnast whose specialty is tumbling. Joyce, a gymnast, specializes in tumbling.

DAY 126: 1. Marco, I've, Citrustime 2. One woman spoke about calves, lambs, and colts at a ranchers' meeting. 3. He <u>lay</u> <s>on the bed</s> and <u>yawned</u>. 4. children's puppy 5. AMV/RA: When we went to the circus, we saw a lion jump through a ring. We saw a lion jump through a ring at the circus.

DAY 127: 1. My, Drew, University, Tommy 2. No, you're not taking Spencer's snake with you.(!) 3. him 4. A. lighter B. most timid 5. AMV/RA: King Charles II gave William Penn land in America in 1681.

DAY 128: 1. Are, Grapevine, Recreational, Area 2. Sarah's first teacher, I think, was Miss Dow. 3. The <u>girl</u> and her <u>dog</u> <u>run</u> <s>before dinner</s>. 4. er 5. AMV/RA: Both his grandfather and his grandmother work for a computer company. His grandfather and grandmother work for computer companies.

DAY 129: 1. A. Hill, Fire B. All, Summer, Day C. Pigs, Might, Fly 2. Is one-third of the woman's doll collection from London, England? 3. <u>leader</u> <u>rose</u>, <u>waved</u>; conjunction = and 4. do, am, was, should, may, had, will, might, were, did, would, are, were 5. AMV/RA: The play will begin at eight o'clock in the auditorium. The eight o'clock play will be held in the auditorium.

DAY 130: 1. The, Dads, Tots, Club, Grandparent's, Day 2. Yes, several mice's tails were curly. 3. more excitedly 4. <u>lady</u> <u>eats</u> 5. AMV/RA: Although the sky was blue in the morning, it rained in the afternoon. The sky was blue in the morning, but it rained in the afternoon.

DAY 131: 1. A, Hindu, New, Delhi, India 2. Wow! We did it, Bobby! 3. A. calves B. buses C. cries D. bunches E. plants F. waxes 4. Some sheep were moved to a new field.   5. AMV/RA: Penguins waddled across the snow and jumped into the water.   Waddling across the snow, the penguins jumped into the water.*

*Note: *Easy Writing* teaches how to write this sentence pattern.

DAY 132:
1. I. Land travel
    A. Train
    B. Bus
  II. Sea travel
2. A tall, thin man greeted Mrs. Begay and her son.   3. often, there
4. student's name/student's street address/city, state zip code   5. AMV/RA: One of the six kitchen lights is burned out. Only five of the six kitchen lights are burning.

DAY 133:   1. A, Boston, Winston, Hotel, May   2. A. <u>Our Family Tree</u>   B. "I'm Nobody"   C. "Got Those Blues"   D. <u>Space News</u>   3. <u>diver must have broken</u>
4. easily   5. AMV/RA: The barbecued slices of turkey were placed in sandwiches. The turkey in the sandwiches had been sliced and barbecued.

DAY 134:   1. Their, Daytona, Targo, Tire, Company
2.
                    29999 Parkside Circle
                    Braintree, MA   02184
                    Aug. 9, 20--
  Dear Pippa,
      I finally made a three-layer cake. It had coconut and choco-
late frosting.   Your friend,
                                Bart
3. A. AMV/RA: light, bleached, white   B. AMV/RA: dark, colorful   C. pail
4. **do**n't   5. AMV/RA: Cheese is a source of protein, fat, and some minerals.

DAY 135:
1. Over in the meadow,
In the sand in the sun,
Lived an old mother toadie
And her little toadie one.
2. A. "Holiday"   B. "Tale of a Tail"   3. <u>tornado was seen</u>   4. A. _   B. _   C. √
D. _   5. AMV/RA: Their new car is gray with bucket seats and fancy wheels. Their new gray car has bucket seats and fancy wheels.

DAY 136:   1. She, Did   2. On the actor's face, lines had been carefully drawn.   3. A. we'll   B. here's   C. they're   D. haven't   E. wouldn't   F. she's
4. well   5. AMV/RA: The misbehaving child threw herself on the floor and

screamed. The child misbehaved by throwing herself on the floor and screaming.

DAY 137:
1.
                                                        11 **Bow Lane**
                                                        Phoenix, AZ 85015
                                                        December 1, 20--
Dear Cousin Bo,
       I saw **Doby Ranch** last summer when visiting **Flagstaff, Arizona.**
                                                   Sincerely yours,
                                                   Jamie
2. You're the last person to try, Mr. Novack.   **3.** well   **4.** heading
5. AMV/RA: Although the clothes have been in the dryer for thirty minutes, they are still damp.

DAY 138:   **1.** Has, Attorney, Gill, Adams, County, Jail
2. Jack,
    It's not too late for you to join us on Satur-
   day for our riders' club picnic.
                          Mano
3. A. un B. happy C. ness   **4.** <u>She stirred</u>; D.O. = batter   **5.** AMV/RA: A chickadee often swings upside down on a branch to find insects.

DAY 139:   **1.** Was, Cortez, Spaniard, Mexico   **2.** A. ft. B. lb. C. in. D. Gov. E. Rd. F. m   **3.** interjection   **4.** any   **5.** AMV/RA: The first cookbook printed in America was published in 1796 in Connecticut.

DAY 140:   **1.** The, Boston, Tea, Party   **2.** Has someone added two-thirds cup of water to the children's activity dough?   **3.** the, that   **4.** <u>dancer performed</u>, <u>bowed</u>   **5.** AMV/RA: Tad's blue bike, a racer, was a birthday gift. Tad's blue racer bike was a birthday gift.

DAY 141:   **1.** They, Mexican, Miracle, Market
2.   I. Famous airplanes
         A. <u>Spirit of St. Louis</u>
         B. <u>Spruce Goose</u>
   II. Famous ships
3. Some (trees), seven (planters)   **4.** <u>(You) Smile</u>   **5.** AMV/RA: The old, gold coin is valuable. The valuable, gold coin is old.*

*Note: This is a good place to emphasize that a comma is used between two adjectives placed side by side unless one is a color or a number. Here <u>gold</u> refers to metal content, not to a color. (There are other exceptions, but this explanation will suffice at this point.)

DAY 142: 1. The, Jewish, Israel, Red, Sea   2. Have you, Connie, ever been to a fiddlers' contest?   3. <u>kitten</u> <u>must have drunk</u>   4. Seven (cows), hungry (cows), the (grass), green (grass), leafy (grass)   5. AMV/RA: Before crossing the street, the child looked both ways. The child first looked both ways and then crossed the street.

DAY 143: 1. Is, U., S., Naval, Supply, Center, Colonial, Parkway   2. Dad's company is located at 42 Dee Rd., Atlanta, Georgia 30345.   3. harder   4. A. interrogative B. declarative C. exclamatory   5. AMV/RA: Brian was watching a history show on television.

DAY 144: 1. A, Fair, Grounds, Smithsonian, Institution   2. Cindy exclaimed, "You're the best!"   3. A. _ B. √ C. √   4. well   5. AMV/RA: An excited boy rushed through the crowd and shouted to his friend.   Rushing through the crowd, an excited boy shouted to his friend.*

*__Note:__ This pattern is taught is *Easy Writing*.

DAY 145: 1. His, Their, Hancock, House, Maryland   2. A light, cool breeze blew through those campers' site.   3. prettier   4. A. present B. future C. past   5. AMV/RA: Wrap Tara's present in blue paper and add a white bow.

DAY 146: 1. An, Atlanta, Memorial, Hospital, Tuesday   2. Have you, Tony, ever heard of a plane called <u>Sky King</u>?   3. A. book B. tape D. bird E. canary   4. A. You're B. their C. it's D. there E. Too   5. AMV/RA: Jim's sunglasses are on the tiled counter.

DAY 147: 1. Last, Captain, Doug, Bayn, Astrodome, Houston   2. "I love it!" exclaimed Nicki.   3. <u>horse</u> <u>ate</u>; D.O. = apple   4. A. run(s), ran, (had) run B. eat(s), ate, (had) eaten C. see(s), saw, (had) seen   5. AMV/RA: Lori and her grandmother took a trip to England.   Lori went with her grandmother to England.

DAY 148: 1. The, Senator, Gert, San, Francisco   2. Kari said, "The guest speaker for the hikers' club has arrived."   3. A. she B. us C. me   4. A. wolves B. irises C. stables D. libraries C. crashes F. volleys   5. AMV/RA: The friendly St. Bernard dog often jumps over the fence.   The friendly dog, a St. Bernard, often jumps over the fence.

DAY 149: 1. The, Anna, Little, Ones, Riverview, Theater   2. Mary's dad, her uncle, and her cousin went to Bangor, Maine.   3. <u>Many</u> ~~of the flowers~~ <u>have</u> already <u>bloomed</u>.   4. very, rather   5. AMV/RA: Heidi's bicycle was in the school's driveway.   The bicycle in the school's driveway belongs to Heidi.

DAY 150: 1. Does, March, Dimes, Association, Easter   2. AMV/RA: Jefferson, Thomas   3. A. √ B. _ C. _ D. _ E. √ F. √   4. well
5. AMV/RA: Ms. Sax is repairing the broken copy machine that has a paper jam. Ms. Sax is repairing the paper jam in the copy machine.

DAY 151: 1. Is, Tournament, Roses, Parade, Pasadena   2. I need the following items for my project: a glue wand, a shirt, and twenty-six stars.   3. Mandy, pens, pencils, notebook   4. (a) sudden (b) supply (c) truth (d) tub
5. AMV/RA: Lemons, limes, oranges, grapefruit, and kumquats are citrus fruits.

DAY 152: 1. Jina, China, Buddhistic
2.
                    957 S. Iron Street
                    Broomall, PA 19008
                    December 31, 20--

Dear Ryan,

      Capt. Lewis and I will arrive at 5:00 next Thursday, January 5.

                    Always,
                    Mario

3. A. heading B. greeting (salutation) C. body D. closing E. signature
4. quietly   5. AMV/RA: The liver is an organ that helps the body in over five hundred ways.

DAY 153: 1. An, Dr., Lang, Smith, Medical, Building   2. "My father," said Kala, "is a good cook."   3. A. speak(s), spoke, (had) spoken B. bring(s), brought, (had) brought C. wear(s), wore, (had) worn   4. AMV/RA: No! Fabulous! Wow! Yeah!   5. AMV/RA: Dr. Jobe is a veterinarian who vaccinates our cows. Dr. Jobe, a veterinarian, vaccinates our cows.

DAY 154: 1. Are, Sierra, Madre, Mountains, Verde, River   2. The ladies' food booth, without a doubt, will be popular.   3. A. √ B. _ C. √   4. in the white house, O.P. = house; on that lane, O.P. = lane   5. AMV/RA: Either Daren or his sister will take Mrs. Gerb to the doctor's office.

DAY 155: 1. Paul, April, Fool's, Day, English, Carter, Elementary, School
2. Yes, our children's chorus sang "Daisy" during their show.   3. Rory's plates
4. A. AMV/RA: needy B. AMV/RA: wealthy, fertile C. pour   5. AMV/RA: The lady in the grocery store screamed because her purse had been stolen. The lady in the grocery store screamed that her purse had been stolen.

DAY 156: 1. Later, Judge, Worth, U., S., Capitol   2. The three-pronged fork, I believe, is in that drawer.   3. ~~At a company picnic~~, her mom <u>grilled</u> hot dogs and <u>served</u> lemonade.   4. A. gloves B. Markin Theater C. Anderson House

Restaurant   D. movie theater   **5**. AMV/RA: Doug's brother is working as a waiter at a newly-opened restaurant. Doug's brother, a waiter, works at a restaurant that just opened.

DAY 157:   **1**. Did, Admiral, Jones, President, Ford, Camp, David   **2**. Did you see the sleek, new boats, Cindy?   **3**. A. _ B. √ C. _ D. _ E. √ F. _ G. √ H. _ I. _   **4**. A. <u>F</u> B. <u>F</u> C. <u>S</u>   **5**. AMV/RA: The stained, wooden floors need to be sanded. The floors that are wooden and stained need to be sanded.

DAY 158:
1.
>15900 **R**ockland **R**oad
>**W**ilmington, **DE** 19803
>**M**ay 12, 20--

>Dear **L**uis,
>   **O**ur club will visit the **D**allas **M**useum of **A**rt in **T**exas. **I** hope to see a painting by **C**. **M**attson.

>   Best wishes,
>   **D**ena

2. Missy asked, "Aren't my shoes' heels too high?"   **3**. The <u>director</u> and her <u>crew</u> <u>filmed</u> the movie <s>at night</s>.   **4**. Eventually, inside   **5**. AMV/RA: After three hours of hiking into a canyon, the group ate lunch.

DAY 159:
1. I. Flags
         A. Country
         B. State and local
     II. Banners
2. A. <u>If You Give a Pig a Pancake</u>   B. "The Potato Soup"   C. <u>The Wizard of Oz</u>
3. most active   **4**. A. imperative B. interrogative   **5**. AMV/RA: Although Amanda talks loudly, Amanda's sister is very quiet. Amanda talks loudly, but her sister is very quiet.

DAY 160:   **1**. Does, Lincoln, Memorial, Dutch   **2**. <u>Old Ironsides</u> is the nickname of a ship in Boston, Massachusetts.   **3**. A. <u>C</u> B. <u>C</u> C. A D. <u>C</u> E. <u>A</u> F. <u>A</u>   **4**. me   **5**. AMV/RA: Sherry purchased a bag of unsalted popcorn. Sherry purchased unsalted popcorn in a bag.

DAY 161:   **1**. Free, Metro, Mall, Wednesday, Mr., Vargas   **2**. During the party, time was spent planning a trip to Paris, France.   **3**. students name/student's street address/student's town (city), state zip code   **4**. A. mustn't B. you'll C. I'd D. can't E. who's F. wouldn't   **5**. AMV/RA: Dark clouds rolled in, and rain fell for an hour. After dark clouds rolled in, rain fell for an hour.

DAY 162:
1. In a shoe box stuffed in an old nylon stocking
   Sleeps the baby mouse I found in the meadow
2. A. <u>Suzanne</u> B. <u>Titanic</u> C. "Writing" 3. mother, dad <u>race</u> 4. A. re B. do C. ing 5. AMV/RA: The white speeding car is dented. The white dented car was speeding.

DAY 163: 1. Micah, In, June, Mom, Lake, Mohawk, New, Jersey 2. "Today," said Maria, "isn't Tuesday." 3. A (fox), quick (fox), brown (fox), the (dog), lazy (dog) 4. Suddenly, hard 5. AMV/RA: The air is filled with smoke because a brush fire is burning.

DAY 164: 1. Hunters, Asia, Bering, Strait, B., C. 2. Mr. and Mrs. Jacobs sell the following: yogurt, ice cream, and milk. 3. more frequently 4. A. smile(s), smiled, (had) smiled B. go/goes, went, (had) gone C. grow(s), grew, (had) grown 5. AMV/RA: Before lunch, they shopped at a factory outlet and bought sweaters. Shopping at a factory outlet before lunch, they bought sweaters.

DAY 165: 1. A. The, Tale, Peter, Rabbit B. From, Seed, Plant C. Gumdrop, Has, Birthday
2. Allie,
   You're invited to attend a writers' breakfast on Tuesday, June 5.
                     Nikko
3. possessive pronoun = his; antecedent = boy 4. <u>Sal</u> <u>will go</u> ~~down the elevator with Jerry~~. 5. AMV/RA: Even though a security guard searched the parking lot for a stolen wallet, he did not find it. The security guard searched the parking lot for a stolen wallet, but it was not found.

DAY 166: 1. For, Canadian, Crispy's 2. The answer, I think, isn't twenty-three, Dakota. 3. Conj. = and; Intj. = Terrific! 4. do, does, did, has, have, had, may, might, must, should, could, would, shall, will, can, is, am, are, was, were, be, being, been 5. AMV/RA: No one helped the lady wash her new car. The lady washed her new car by herself.

DAY 167: 1. Mrs., Dil, Adams, Junior, High, School, West, Log, Street 2. Ouch! Those cacti's stickers are sharp! 3. together, well 4. possessive pronoun = their; antecedent = neighbors 5. AMV/RA: Juan put onions, mustard, and pickles on the hot dog that he bought. After buying a hot dog, Juan put onions, mustard, and pickles on it.

DAY 168: 1. Is, Fingal's, Cave, Staffa, Island, Scotland
2. I. Mountains
    A. Rockies

              B. Appalachians
        II. Rivers
              A. Colorado
              B. Rio Grande
3. children's pig   **4.** Two (ladies), young (ladies), that (boat), sinking (boat)
5. AMV/RA: The grass is brown because it hasn't rained recently. Because it hasn't rained recently, the grass is brown.

DAY 169:   **1.** Marsha, Did, Buckingham, Palace
2.   2 Doe Street
                                                Scottsdale, Arizona 85254
                                                March 7, 20--

    Dear Ed,
           How are you doing? We'll see you in a few months. (!)
                                                Your friend,
                                                Danno
3. A. heading   B. greeting (salutation) C. body D. closing E. signature
4. Two <u>crocks</u> and a wire <u>basket</u> <u>are</u> ~~under the workbench~~.   **5.** AMV/RA:
Although his blue lunch box is shaped like a radio, it doesn't play music. His blue lunch box shaped like a radio doesn't play music.

DAY 170:   **1.** In, Spanish, Inca, Indians, Peru   **2.** Does Josh live at 34 Route 10, Succasunna, NJ 07876?   **3.** A. to, too B. their C. you're D. Can E. it's
4. so, not   **5.** AMV/RA: Joel made a paper airplane and flew it across the room. Having made a paper airplane, Joel flew it across the room.

DAY 171:   **1.** Their, Bee, Rock, Campground, Christmas, Eve   **2.** A. "Your Muscles" B. <u>Benji</u> C. <u>Home Redo</u>   **3.** A. risen B. set C. lying D. lay
4. They, their   **5.** AMV/RA: Myra joined an expensive fitness center yesterday. Although the fitness center that opened yesterday is expensive, Myra joined.

DAY 172:   **1.** Does, Halo, Hair, Salon, Beach, Boulevard, Mrs., Wong
2. "You're the best," the man announced, "in this division."   **3.** A. <u>cowboy must have gone</u> B. <u>lawyer has brought</u> C. <u>We should have seen</u>   **4.** most slowly
5. AMV/RA: The bicyclist stopped and rested on a park bench.

DAY 173:   **1.** Is, Babe, Ruth's, National, Baseball, Hall, Fame, Museum, Cooperstown   **2.** Ebony asked, "Where's Dora's note pad?"   **3.** (upper left corner) student's name/student's street address/city, state zip code; (middle of envelope) friend's name/friend's street address/city, state zip code   **4.** and, but
5. AMV/RA: The engraved, silver belt buckle belongs to a rancher.* The rancher's silver belt buckle is engraved.

*Note: This is a good place to emphasize that a comma is used between two adjectives placed side by side unless one is a color or a number. In this sentence, <u>silver</u> refers to a metal, not to a color.

DAY 174: 1. Rick, Fort, Ticonderoga, American, Revolution   2. Wow! I've jumped nearly four feet, Mrs. Moreno!   3. <u>We ate, drank</u>; D.O. - doughnuts, juice   4. A. doesn't B. we're C. who's D. they're E. didn't F. I'm   5. AMV/RA: After Joe walked to the drugstore, he purchased gumdrops, licorice, and crackers. When Joe walked to the drugstore, he purchased gumdrops, licorice, and crackers.

DAY 175: 1. Chad, Sharp, Music, Supply   2. A. <u>Fiddler on the Roof</u> B. <u>Tex</u> C. "Insects" D. "Evangeline"   3. A. memories B. recesses C. traces D. reefs E. mice F. surreys   4. <u>May I open</u> that gate ~~for you~~?   5. AMV/RA: Mrs. Delany is cooking a turkey in an oblong roasting pan. Mrs. Delany's turkey is being roasted in an oblong pan.

DAY 176: 1. Shane, We, Prescott, Music, Festival, July   2. Kala, I must buy these items for our trip: sunblock, a hat, and a beach towel.   3. A. declarative B. exclamatory C. interrogative D. imperative   4. better, best   5. AMV/RA: Although Millie's first answer of five was incorrect, her second answer was right. Millie's first answer of five was incorrect, but her second answer was correct.

DAY 177: 1. During, Hawaiian, Polynesian, Waikiki, Beach   2. Franny asked, "Is our girls' volleyball team playing today?"   3. A. √ B. √ C. _   4. A. <u>F</u> B. <u>S</u> C. <u>S</u> D. <u>F</u> E. <u>S</u> F. <u>F</u>   5. AMV/RA: Salco Corporation on Porter Avenue makes car mirrors. Salco Corporation, located on Porter Avenue, makes car mirrors.

DAY 178: 1. A. Prairie, Sisters B. An, Apple, Colliwobble C. Barry, Has, Fright   2. Lynn Batt
   12 Trow St.
   Plano, Texas 75074

          Mr. and Mrs. Bob L. Suite
          Post Office Box 25601
          Eagle Ridge, NY 12057

3. door, house, patio   4. AMV/RA: total, complete   5. AMV/RA: The cookies that he made have chunks of chocolate and peanuts. He made cookies containing peanuts and chunks of chocolate.

DAY 179: 1. His, Uncle, Gil, Arabian, Santa, Fe, New, Mexico   2. The men's club will perform a short, funny musical at 8:00.   3. A. they're B. its C. Your D. too   4. Yesterday, down, very, clumsily   5. AMV/RA: Please pick up the bird book that is on the floor. A book about birds is on the floor; please pick it up.*

*Note: This construction is taught in *Easy Writing*.

DAY 180:
1.
                                                10 Brak Lane
                                                Chelsea, MI 48118
                                                December 12, 20--

Dear Ricardo,
      We're looking forward to visiting Shelter Island, the zoo, and a Mexican food restaurant.
                                                Your pal,
                                                Shelly

2. Tara's mother needs ice, lemons, and sugar to make the drink.   3. A. heading B. greeting (salutation) C. body D. closing E. signature   4. more eager
5. AMV/RA: While Taley's parents went to Ohio, Taley stayed with her aunt.